PLAYHOUSE
Six Fantasy Plays for Children

Edited by
JOYCE DOOLITTLE

Northern Lights Books for Children
Red Deer College Press

Acknowledgments
The publishers extend special thanks to Joyce Doolittle, whose dedication to children's
theatre made this book possible; to designers Tara Ryan, Douglas McCullough and
James Andrews, who gave so freely of their time and talent; and to Norman Barr,
Vicki Mix and Patrica Roy, who generously assisted in the preparation of this book.
The publishers gratefully acknowledge the financial assistance of the Alberta
Foundation of the Literary Arts, Alberta Culture and Multiculturalism, the Canada
Council and Radio 7 CKRD.

Credits
Edited by Joyce Doolittle
Cover design by Terry Leonard, Gallery Graphics
Typeset by Boldface Technologies Ltd.
Printed and bound in Canada by the Jasper Printing Group
for Red Deer College Press

Canadian Cataloguing in Publication Data
Main entry under title:
Playhouse: six fantasy plays for children
(Northern lights books for children)
Contents: Prairie dragons / Sharon Pollock – Friends / Tom Bentley-Fisher – A nest of
dragons / Zina Barnieh – The old woman and the pedlar / Betty Jane Wylie – The
merchants of Dazu / James DeFelice – Swimmers / Clem Martini
ISBN 0-88995-028-8
1. Children's plays, Canadian (English).*
I. Doolittle, Joyce, 1928- II. Series.
PS8307.P43 1989 jC812'.54'0809282
PR9196.7.C48P43 1989 C88-091146-8

Contents

Preface

"In order to master the psychological problems of growing up – overcoming narcissistic disappointments, oedipal dilemmas, sibling rivalries; becoming able to relinquish childhood dependencies; gaining a feeling of selfhood and of self-worth, and a sense of moral obligation – a child needs to understand what is going on within his conscious self so that he can also cope with that which goes on in his unconscious. He can achieve this understanding, and with it the ability to cope, not through rational comprehension of the nature and content of his unconscious, but by becoming familiar with it through spinning out daydreams – ruminating, rearranging, and fantasizing about suitable story elements in response to unconscious pressures. By doing this, the child fits unconscious content into conscious fantasies, which then enable him to deal with that content" (Bruno Bettleheim, *The Uses Of Enchantment*).

Fantasy is one way of dealing with reality that has its roots deep in the human psyche. The sources of fantasy spring from the human imagination and give us the means to express the inexpressible and to identify ourselves and our place in the world through myths, archetypes and icons. To a child, fantasy is sometimes more real than the real thing. The fantasy elements in these six plays are varied: Dragons fly in *A Nest of Dragons*; dragon tracks are discovered in *Prairie Dragons*; characters as old as the *commedia dell'arte* – the doctor, the pedlar, the mime among them – confront the heroine of *The Old Woman and the Pedlar* as personifications of her hopes and despairs. The most elemental of the elements – water – is a major character in *Swimmers*: first as a dream of escape, then as a force to fear and ultimately as a realm to respect. The unreasonable and selfish fantasies of its leading characters propel the plot of *The Merchants of Dazu* and it is immensely satisfying to see their greed and avarice punished. The boys and girls in *Friends* create unique personal spaces which they imagine into other worlds, and the vigil of the duck eggs in the daycare brings them into direct contact with the ultimate mysteries of birth and death.

A specialized theatre for children is less than one hundred years old. It began in Russia before the revolution when a young actress, Natalia Sats, decided to make producing plays for boys and girls her life's work. Professional theatre for children in Canada began only after World War II with the establishment of Holiday Theatre in Vancouver, British Columbia, in 1953. Canada's theatre for the young is now vigorous and varied. In its early days, plays were chosen from England, the United States and France, but today the largest percentage of scripts are written by Canadians. These six plays have been chosen to reflect the diversity of style, which is one of the glories of the genre in Canada, as well as for their inclusion of fantasy.

Three scripts in *Playhouse* draw upon traditional material. *A Nest of Dragons* is an old fairy tale which Zina Barnieh remembered as a favourite from her Italian childhood. When Calgary's Quest Theatre commissioned a new script, she used it as her source. Also, as the mother of three children, she was also interested in perennial problems of childhood. *A Nest of Dragons* became the first play in a trilogy – each inspired by one of her three children. *A Nest of Dragons* is dedicated to Dean, her oldest child and only son. It is a journey play in which a passion of childhood is transformed through trials into a more adult attachment and attitude. In the manner of many fairy tales, the hero's virtues and vices are personified and an actual physical confrontation symbolizes his inner psychic struggle.

Betty Jane Wylie's *The Old Woman and the Pedlar* is based upon a nursery rhyme. The story is deceptively simple – even silly. On her way home from the market, an old woman falls asleep beside the road. A pedlar mischievously cuts off her skirts as she sleeps. When she awakens, she looks so different to herself that she is not sure of her own identity. She devises a test. If her little dog at home barks at her, she is someone else. He does. Now, who is she? Her search for a name and an identity form the material for Ms. Wylie's play. Most people have had a dramatic change of circumstance sometime in their lives which disturbed their sense of themselves. And children, subject to rapid growth and not having direct control over many aspects of their everyday living, feel this unease frequently.

In *The Merchants of Dazu*, James DeFelice tells a story of human greed and its comeuppance with devices used in the oriental theatre. There are also echoes of Berthold Brecht in the minimal scenery and in the social message of the play. Audience satisfaction is enhanced by the classic structure of the play, which repeats the outward journey in reverse and allows the audience the delicious anticipation of the villains' punishment.

In an ingenious combination of tradition and modernity, Sharon Pollock's *Prairie Dragons* takes place in the past but is written with a completely contemporary sensibility. The two heroines face prejudice and adversity with resourcefulness and courage. The play combines documentary techniques with devices of the oriental theatre and also includes choral speaking, poetry and an audacious premise: that ancient dragons have accompanied Chinese immigrants and dug into the prairie soil to make old paths in a new world.

Swimmers, by Clem Martini, is set in the present. Most of its scenes are realistic depictions of family and school life. The fantasy is in the dream shared by Wendy and Lyle, a dream of an endless body of water where they swim to their heart's content. Like "Never Never Land" in Peter Pan, the water represents a place where adult rules do not apply and where one's own prowess (literally) keeps one afloat.

Tom Bentley-Fisher's *Friends* is the most realistic of the six plays. Set in a daycare centre and based upon the author's observation of his own child in similar circumstances, the fantasy element in *Friends* occurs within the imagination of each child and is made manifest in the unique environment each creates with the boxes which dominate the set. The miracle of birth is another vital ingredient in *Friends*. The duck eggs are omnipresent throughout the play and the wonder of birth affects each member of the daycare – individually and as a caring constituency.

The theatre is a fantasy even when the circumstances of an individual script are realistic. Each play is a world of its own, creating conventions within conventions. The imagining of individual minds is one of the glories of reading, but scenes must take tangible shape when a script moves from the page to the stage.

Collaboration between a director and a designer or a team of designers is professional theatre's way of creating a world convincing for the actors and the audience while remaining true to the author's intention. Because I have had some of my most exciting times in the process of playmaking as a director collaborating with designers, I have asked several of my colleagues to put their design solutions on paper so that the reader may see that there are many ways to solve problems posed by playwrights.

The sketches, drawings and comments which appear in *Playhouse* represent some of the kinds of creative responses that working designers make to the text of a play. The range of style and execution varies. For *A Nest of Dragons*, Douglas McCullough has contributed detailed drawings to solve one of the main images presented by the playwright: flying on the backs of dragons. For *The Merchants of Dazu*, the central metaphor of the journey has been encapsulated in McCullough's rendering of the continuously painted screen concept. Anyone who wants to produce *Merchants* is urged to consult authentic Chinese painting styles for inspiration on specific scenes for the curtain. The hardest problem to solve in staging *Swimmers* is how to put swimming actors on stage so that the audience is convinced that they are actually in water. Douglas McCullough has designed and drawn one way by which this could be accomplished. James Andrews has suggested simple solutions for lighting *Swimmers*, a play in which light and sound can make important contributions to the total effect of the performance. For *Prairie Dragons*, the reader or prospective producer is offered McCullough's 'dragonscape.' Tara Ryan has taken a different approach in *Friends* and *The Old Woman and the Pedlar*, providing 'doodles' characteristic of many designers' first reading response to a script. Quenten Doolittle's music for the opening song in *The Old Woman and the Pedlar* is included to show the usefulness of a theme and variations to some plays. This particular tune was used extensively in the first production, in various musical styles and send-ups, with many created on the synthesizer.

Contemporary playwrights who want to see their work produced professionally must write for small casts. There are seldom more than five actors in an Equity touring company. Various techniques to suggest more characters have been developed by writers. Sharon Pollock uses cutout figures for Mr. Whitherspoon, Johnny Whitherspoon and Mrs. Kwong. In *A Nest of Dragons*, Zina Barnieh suggests using puppets for the crowd of commoners who act as a chorus and comment upon the actions of royalty. An orthodox, predictable response given by puppets makes a strong statement, but the chorus of commoners could be played by live actors. To indicate conformity, another kind of stylization would be necessary – an exaggerated method of speaking, for example, or identical costumes, or both. When my university class in Theatre for Children produced *Friends*, we used a human calendar. Two mimes and a musician (in our production it was a flautist) developed routines for each calendar change and were a popular feature of the performance. We also had many people present at the birth of the ducks. They said live what the authors had indicated in the script as recorded. Caution in amending the author's material is essential, but techniques invented to cut costs for professional productions are not always appropriate in educational institutions where significant participation for each student is often an important goal.

Reading a play can be a satisfying experience; seeing a play is even more powerful; but performing in a play or being part of a production team is the most potent of all. I hope that all three opportunities will occur as a result of the publication of this anthology. I believe in the value of live theatre – not as an outmoded or quaint relic from "the olden days" but as a significant alternative to television – one with ancient powers leading to deep personal experiences.

Joyce Doolittle, Calgary, Alberta

A Nest of Dragons
ZINA BARNIEH

Design Concept by Douglas McCullough

ZINA BARNIEH was born in Udine, Italy, and immigrated to Canada as a child. She received her Master of Fine Arts in Theatre Studies from the University of Victoria and taught drama at the University of Calgary. She has written eight plays for children, all of which have been produced by Calgary theatres. Zina Barnieh is also the coauthor, with Joyce Doolittle, of *A Mirror of Our Dreams: Children and Theatre in Canada* (Talonbooks, 1979). She is currently actively researching and writing about playwriting and drama in education.

A Nest of Dragons was first produced by Quest Theatre, Calgary, Alberta, May 4, 1985, with the following cast:

Andy Curtis
Ralamy Kneeshaw
Brendan Lavery
Deborah Miller
James Downey
Barbara Campbell-Brown

Directed and Designed by Duval Lang

CHARACTERS
Queen of Italy
Midwife (Actress can double as Princess)
Princess
Tutor
Commoners (Rod puppets attached)
Prince of Italy
Ambassador (Actor can double as Escort)
Escort
Princesses of Germany, France, and Spain (Same Actress, different hats)
Dragons (Actors and/or projected shadows on a wall)
Baby Dragons (Hand puppets in a nest)

Costumes and props are on stage during the entire play. Actors are seen to play double roles and stay on stage during the play.

A Nest of Dragons

Tutor: This story was told, then written in ink.
To know if it's true look inside and think.
Long ago in the Kingdom of Italy
A widowed queen expects her first baby.
For this royal mom a great event,
Now there'd be an heir heaven sent.

> *Curtain hides Queen in labour. Midwife helping her. Tutor is pacing. Midwife runs out.*

Midwife: I had a premonition when I saw that full moon up there. I said to myself, "It's going to be another busy night for you."

Queen: Midwife, where are you?

Midwife: Be right there, Your Highness.

Tutor: The poor widowed queen and no husband to help her.

> *Sounds of newborn cats made by actors.*

Is it…?

> *Midwife peeking from behind curtain.*

Midwife: No, Sir, the mother cat and kittens.

Tutor: Oh, yes, kittens…

> *Sounds of kid.*

Finally, it's happened…

Midwife: No, Sir, that was the nanny goat…

Tutor: Yes, a kid…

> *Human baby sounds. He paces faster. Freezes.*

Midwife: Dear Sir, a prince is born!

> *She carries out baby.*

Thanks be to God.

Tutor: A Prince! Thanks be to God. The royal Mother must be proud? And the King, God rest his soul, must be looking down from heaven and smiling. You shall grow up to be the next king. Sweet thing.

Queen: (*walks out*) Let us say prayers of thanks.

> *Shuts eyes and prays.*

Midwife: Ahem!

                Whispers to Tutor.

Tutor: The fee, Your Majesty!

Queen: Oh, yes, the fee.

                Pulls money discreetly out of bra.

                Here you go. Where was I?

                Resumes praying.

Midwife: Ahem!

Tutor: Your Greatness, and for the goat?

Queen: Oh, yes, for the goat. Here you are.

                Prays.

                Midwife impatient.

Tutor: There was also the cat, Your Generosity.

Queen: Oh, all right, the cat too.

                *Midwife bows and exits counting money. Noting she's gone the
                Queen opens her eyes.*

                We'll plan the grandest christening. Invite the courts of
                Germany, France and Spain.

Tutor: And Austria?

Queen: Not Austria, they didn't invite us to their wedding, not very
                neighbourly, would you say?

Tutor: I'll tell the Royal Secretary to send invitations.

Queen: I suppose the commoners want to celebrate, too. They were
                spoiled by my poor husband, God rest his soul.

                Crosses herself.

                Plan a party for them in the anteroom, not too expensive. I
                may have to ask a small admission to cover the costs. The royal
                coffers are dwindling

                Hears baby, goat and cat.

                and there are three more mouths to feed.

Commoner 1:   Such a big fuss over one baby. Who fussed over the fourteen
                babies in our house? Oh, but there's only one little baby
                Prince. He'll be so coddled and cuddled that he won't be able
                to do anything to save his life.

Commoner 2:	You know the old saying: Some are born great! Did you hear about the Queen who traced her family tree?
Commoner 1:	No.
Commoner 2:	She found nothing but monkeys in it.

CHILDHOOD

Queen and Tutor are playing croquet.

Queen:	We must interest the Prince in croquet and civilized recreational activities. He's too interested in animals and wild things. That won't do him any good in the royal courts.

She is much better at this game.

Tutor:	He has a good way with animals. Do you know he taught the cat to roll over? It was something to see, the cat sat there and at his signal it went like this –

Demonstrating with glee.

Queen:	Really, Tutor. What use is that? It's time he had a more formal education. His Father would have wanted a private education with fine teachers.
Tutor:	Oh, the finest.
Queen:	And I tried to think what teachers would I trust with my son – teachers that we could afford within our budgetary limitations.
Tutor:	One must be careful these days, with budgets and teachers. Well, you know best.
Queen:	The best Teacher, Protector and Companion that I could think of was right here in this palace.
Tutor:	But I don't know anyone qualified to teach the Prince.
Queen:	Why you! It's you I want as a teacher for my son, to raise as future King. You're all those things I said plus you're right here and already in my service. Saves on the cost.
Tutor:	I'm flattered beyond words. I never expected…and a future King.
Queen:	I expect you to teach him Literature, Mathematics, Religion, Science, and Arts and Sporting activities as benefit a Prince.
Tutor:	I'm not sure that I'm qualified in the Sporting Activities, perhaps another tutor…
Queen:	Don't fret, you can do all that needs doing. Do you want a raise?

Tutor:	It's not the salary Your Bountiful Unexpectedness...it's the skill level...
Queen:	Oh, bother, it's settled. You'll do just fine. It feels good to make decisions...Sports aren't very important anyway.

Exit.

Tutor:	Don't expect me to do much about sports. I can teach him botany, or reading but...

Enter Prince carrying a rope.

Hello, young man, where have you been hiding?

Prince:	I found a nest of eagles in the tallest pine tree.
Tutor:	Are you sure it was eagles, it would be strange to find eagles in the palace gardens, maybe magpies or robins or...
Prince:	Eagles are much larger, I know the difference. I'd love to catch one. I'd tame it and teach it tricks. I'll show you the nest.
Tutor:	Later, later...this morning I have a lesson for you. And you want to learn your lessons well.

Prince sneaks away.

If you learn your botany you can be in charge of the gardens in a few years. The gardens, the rose garden, the China Rose, *Rosa Chinesis,* next the Damask Rose, *Rosa Damascana.* Where are you, where has he gone? He's got to learn his lessons...ah, boys...

Prince:	Look, I've brought some of the broken eggshell to prove it's an eagle, it was on the ground...
Tutor:	Today's lesson isn't eggshells, it's roses, the Damask Rose, say "*Rosa Damascana,*" sit still now...
Prince:	The eagle circled the nest, it didn't take its eyes off me.
Tutor:	Eagles, eggshells, concentrate! Name the different rose species.
Prince:	Could we raise eagles in our greenhouse?
Tutor:	Tame your imagination...there are no eagles here, they're wild birds, anyway the greenhouse isn't large enough, and they can be very dangerous.
Prince:	Newly hatched eaglets don't hurt people.
Tutor:	They don't remain newly hatched, they grow into wild eagles.

Prince:	I want to try raising them. I don't care if it's not done.
Tutor:	What reason is there for raising eagles? They can't sing like canaries or talk like parrots.
Prince:	I want to watch them grow up and tame them.
Tutor:	Enough fantasy, some things are naturally wild, you'll understand when you grow up. Now, the roses…
Commoner 1:	What can you expect from a spoiled only child? Eagles for pets. He should be happy with his horses, goats and cats.
Commoner 2:	He's his Father's son. Did you hear about the prince who traced his family tree?
Commoner 1:	Tell me.
Commoner 2:	He found out he was the sap.

MOTHER AND SON

Prince sneaks up behind Mother and puts his hands over her eyes.

Prince:	*(goat sounds)* MMMMAAAA mmmmaaaa. Guess who.
Queen:	My favourite goat, of course.
Prince:	*(imitates tutor)* Wrong, Your Majestic Beauty, someone much wiser.
Queen:	My son's teacher, very easy to guess. I've been wanting to talk to you about being tougher with that boy, more disciplined.
Prince:	Wrong again, it's the amazing boy who can astound you with great skills in archery! Never seen in all of Europe, perhaps the entire world, now before your very eyes he will…

Mimes shooting.

Bull's-eye.

Queen:	I've heard about your interest with the bow and arrow. Waste of time.
Prince:	I practice every spare minute I get, come and watch.
Queen:	First, I have a surprise.
Tutor:	More new schoolbooks?
Queen:	Shut *your* eyes. Put out your hands, open your hands, now open your eyes.

She places a new bow and arrow in his hands.

Prince:	My very own!…Look at the wood. It's better than any bow I've

used before.

Hugs her and gets everything tangled up with bow, Queen and self.

Thank you.

Queen: Be careful, son, I don't want anyone hurt.

Prince: I'll be the most careful archer in the world. And when I hunt...ah, yes

He's both the hunter and the hunted.

here is the world famous hunter, tracking the biggest, wildest, meanest bear in the forest. Hunt, hunt, hunt. I see the bear... come up behind him...downwind...trek, trek, trek...he doesn't know I'm here...suddenly the wind changes...he smells me...sniff, sniff, sniff...AHA...I shoot him, a shot so accurate he's instantly killed. The beast dies. AAARRRGGGHHH. Arrgghh. Argh.

Queen: *(melodramatically)* And I, his poor bear Mother, run over and mourn...ah, ah, my poor bear son, those cruel wicked hunters, who so cruelly stalk us, murdered you in cold blood. Woe to us who are the hunted.

Prince: You're spoiling it, Mother. You're spoiling the whole hunt by crying like that. Be brave, like me.

Queen: Some of us have to think of the consequences of the hunt.

Prince: Mothers!

Stomps away.

ADOLESCENCE

Prince: Tutor, look at my brand new bow, larger and quicker than that toy one I used to have.

Tutor: Looks a little large for a little man.

Prince: Not at all! I can handle this easily. And I can catch real animals instead of just practicing.

Tutor: Catch animals, wait a minute. I won't teach you that.

Prince: You don't have to, I've got all the instructions from the master archer in town on handling this bow and my hunting. The grasp is like this. He told me to watch the angle of the meeting point of the bow and arrow. It's very important. And he said, "Concentration is all."

	Shoots.
	Look at that!
Tutor:	You're a natural, no doubt about it.
Prince:	Foot position is important. And concentration.
	Shoots again.
	Even closer.
Tutor:	You learn this faster than you learn your botany.
Prince:	*(shoots)* Bull's-eye! If at first you don't succeed…practice! I could do this all day.
Tutor:	You're talented, no doubt about it, but a balanced education is best!
Prince:	I want to hunt on the summit, I'm tired of the forests near here.
Tutor:	Oh, child, the wild ideas you come up with. You're the only son and heir to the throne, you have to look after you're own safety first and foremost.
Prince:	I'm not a baby, I know what I'm doing. I'm going to ask Mother about this. Boys my age have gone on big hunts before, why not me?
Tutor:	You're not just any boy.

Prince exits.

Oh, I hope that she doesn't blame me for his wild ideas. It wasn't my doing. I've given him the best curriculum, quiet study, a gentle manner. But he's always been fascinated by the wild animals…never the flowers or the pet canaries…no it's the falcons, the boars and the wild bears. Natural instinct…

HUNTING

Queen:	Why?
Prince:	Why not?
Queen:	It's been a hobby, not something for you to take seriously. There's no need. A little hunting here and there, but the summit? No!
Prince:	I've heard stories about the hunts on the summit.
Queen:	Couldn't you take a little more interest in staff supervision, finances…that's more suitable for a son of mine.

Tutor:	I've tried to tell him, but sometimes there's no accounting for natural inclinations.
Prince:	And I'm good at hunting. During a hunt, in the thickest part of the forest, at the end of the day, I was ready to give up, to turn around and come home. When I least expected it, I heard a loud rustling sound ahead of us. My friends wanted to turn back, but I was more curious than ever. I moved ahead slowly, carefully, when all of a sudden, in the dusk, glaring at me with eyes like fire: a wild boar! Quickly, I let one arrow fly, it hit the beast, but it started coming toward me. Then I let fly a second arrow, and with the third the blood rushed in a stream, and it collapsed.
Queen:	Spare me any more details.
Prince:	And that was only a wild boar, they say there are bears if we go further onto the summit. Imagine a bear skin.
Queen:	His Father never hunted, why him?
Tutor:	No two trees grow alike, Your Highness.
Prince:	I need a new challenge.
Queen:	You can take an interest in a new sport, spend more time with the horses.
Prince:	Horses? I need new territory to hunt. I want to climb the summit.
Queen:	The summit? Tuto, you're an intelligent man, tell me how many hunters have come back from the summit wounded or crippled, or do not return at all? We need you alive and healthy.
Tutor:	Very good point, Your Majesty. The Hostler and the Butcher were very unfortunately maimed, it was such a tragic…
Prince:	Tuto, you're an intelligent man, tell me how many hunters have come back in perfect health.
Tutor:	Well there's the Ironmonger, he had a thrilling tale to tell…
Prince:	And dear Tuto, wasn't one of your greatest lessons to me that I trust myself to know what's right for me? Quote, "Natural instinct and common sense can be your trusted guide," unquote.
Tutor:	I did say that, yes, and what I meant was…
Prince:	What you meant was I trust myself. And I think you should trust me.

Queen:	But he also meant that an older person has more experience and better common sense than a younger one to know when a journey is life threatening.
Prince:	On the one hand, I'm to trust myself, and on the other hand, I'm not old enough to trust myself.
Queen:	Our own forests are dangerous enough without going to the summit. Hunt, if you must, but hunt here. Discussion ended.

Turns her back on the Prince.

Prince:	I've handled any danger that comes my way dozens of times...the boars, the wolf and...

Turns his back on the Queen and walks away.

Tutor:	As you can see we're at an impasse, between a rock and a hard place. Seem familiar? The protective parent pitted against the adventurous child and only heir. Dear, dear, how far does he have to go with these wild things?

Prince is hiding, listening, we can see him.

Queen:	He's been sulking in his rooms, won't take his meals, what a stubborn streak! Don't know where that comes from.
Tutor:	Some call that strength of character.
Queen:	How long does he plan to stay in his rooms?
Tutor:	He's really a sensible boy, ah...young man! Now he has to try his wings, as it were.
Queen:	I will not approve a life-threatening hunt on a distant mountaintop.
Tutor:	He might eventually go on his own without your consent.
Queen:	He doesn't have the money to put together a hunting party.
Tutor:	When a bird wants to fly can you tie down its wings?
Queen:	Would you go along with him...watch him...you're his lifelong friend.
Tutor:	I'm not much for hunting expeditions, Your Gracefulness.
Queen:	You don't have to hunt. He hunts, you watch. And watch he comes home safe and sound.
Tutor:	There's a wonderful experienced guide who would take good care of him, he's just the man to do the job for you. I'll stay here.

Queen:	No, if you go, I'll consider approving it.

Prince jumps out from hiding place.

Prince:	*(Prince gives Mother a kiss, puts his arms around Tutor)* Of course, he'll go. It'll be just like a long walk in the garden, Tuto. You'll love seeing all the new plants and trees up there.
Tutor:	Consider my age, hiking up mountains! Without the comforts of home!
Prince:	I'll arrange for every comfort we can possibly manage.
Tutor:	Now I'm between the rock and hard place!
Prince:	He says "Yes," Mother, let's start getting ready.
Commoner 1:	Good-for-nothing son! If I had a son like that I'd have a good mind to thrash him until he understood what his duty was.
Commoner 2:	What can you expect from a son who's never had to work for a living? Easy come…easy go.
Commoner 1:	Did you hear the one about the prince who had to work for a living?
Commoner 2:	No, I didn't.

THE MOUNTAIN

Sounds of wind, birds, river.

Tutor:	Three days to reach the summit.

Sore back, tired.

As the mountain became steeper, the forest thicker, the prince grew more excited.

To Prince.

Let's sit for a minute and take in the view, the waterfall, the wild flowers, tiny dots of yellow, blue and white. God does have a sense of colour, does he not?

Prince:	We didn't come to sit. We want to reach the top by sundown, let's hurry.
Tutor:	Hurry, hurry, hurry…
Escort:	There's fewer and fewer birds and animals up here.
Tutor:	More alpine flowers. This may not be the best place to hunt.
Prince:	Not many people reach this height, the animals are probably hiding from us. Maybe it's the best hunting.

Escort: It's getting so steep, we'll need the ropes.

Prince: The best approach would be from the southern side.

Tutor: Good, a chance to sit, the sky against the mountainside, a strange, eerie orange and red...

Escort: Quiet up here.

Prince: We're not used to the silence of nature.

> *Great hissing, whistling, uproarious flapping, shadows of dragons appear on screen or wall behind actors.*

Tutor: Dear God.

> *Prays.*

Escort: What is it? It's after us, coming this way.

Prince: *(in awe)* A serpent's body, bat wings as large as a ship.

> *Grabs bow and arrow.*

             I'll get it before it gets us.

> *Shoots.*

Escort: What if you miss, don't try it.

Tutor: Please God, let him succeed on the first try.

Prince: *(shoots)* It's getting too close for comfort. Good. It's down.

Escort: It's only wounded. It could come after us again.

Prince: It should be a mortal wound.

Tutor: A giant, living ship folding its sails.

Escort: *(thud of dragon falling)* Look out. Run. I'll meet you down the hill.

Tutor: Dragons, I've only read about.

Prince: Listen, more...

> *Hissing.*

Tutor: Dear Lord, another one. We've come too far, how many of these creatures are up here?

Prince: Courage, we're safe.

> *Prepares bow.*

Tutor: *(prays)* I've lived a good life, tried to do my duty...

Prince: This one's not as big.

Tutor:	It looks every bit as fierce.
Prince:	*(shoots)* Razed its wing…this one will raze its heart.
Tutor:	What if there are more waiting to take revenge?
Prince:	I've got enough arrows…
Tutor:	What if they outnumber your arrows?
Prince:	Got it this time. Listen, no more.
Tutor:	*(hears dragon babies)* Do they usually live in colonies or mate in twos?
Prince:	I don't know the usual habits of such unusual beasts.
	Babies again.
	SSHHH!
Tutor:	Don't go looking for trouble.
Prince:	Look, it must be their nest, with babies in it, those hungry little tongues.
Tutor:	You're going too far.
Prince:	Or maybe they're calling for their dead Mother and Father…
Tutor:	Are you sure that they're dead? This is not your cat or goat!
Prince:	They can barely hold up their heads, they must be newborn.
	Hears rustling.
Tutor:	Stop, for heaven's sake, what's that sound?
Escort:	What are you waiting for, let's go, there's probably more of them around here, hurry!
Prince:	Just have a short look at the babies.
Tutor:	I'm coming down with you.
Escort:	Animals will attack anything that goes near their young.
Prince:	Not when they're dead. These babies are all alone out here.
Escort:	You're assuming that they're dead. My Mother told me. She said, "You're going off with the wild Prince? Take care, he's not predictable." Well, here we are…and dragons…and…
Prince:	Poor scared things.
Escort:	Poor scared things? I don't believe this.

Prince:	With no one to look after them they might die.
Escort:	Let them die. There must be other dragons nearby, they'll be rescued.
Prince:	I'm taking them alive, nest and all.
Escort:	Taking the vermin alive?
Prince:	Soft, down-covered bodies. Pass some bread.
Escort:	Pass my bread?
Tutor:	That's enough, leave them alone if you have any sense.
Escort:	Do they have teeth? Fiery breath?
Prince:	Fuzzy little heads, wings sprouting like fish fins.
Escort:	I've heard their tongues are poisonous.
Prince:	They're so afraid, but they like me. Some water.
Escort:	My water? My bread and water! My Mother was right!
Prince:	They're curling up to go to sleep. They'll sleep while we hike.
Tutor:	Wait a minute, you're carrying them away from their wilderness?
Prince:	I'm carrying them.
Tutor:	To where?
Prince:	Home.
Tutor & Escort:	Home?
Tutor:	Sit down, the lack of oxygen at this height has affected all of us, I'm sure. Think about it: the palace, the Queen, the staff and…the dragons?…
Prince:	…The dragons…
Tutor:	…And deliver us from evil, Amen.

RAISING THE DRAGONS

Queen:	And how long do you intend to keep these…creatures?
Prince:	They're pets, I'll train them, raise them.
Queen:	Why are you doing this? Maybe if you hadn't grown up with so many animals, you wouldn't have this fascination.

Pause.

These…"pets" will grow to be how large? They're already

eating huge quantities…then there's the cleaning up. Such big messes, really…son…the staff is feeling strained at these new duties added to their already busy tasks.

Prince: They obey, and they're as gentle as any dog. If we're kind to them, they'll be good. I'm interested in seeing if we can take wild creatures and domesticate them. When they're trained, you won't even notice they're around.

Queen: I won't notice the staff living in fear, or the feeding costs growing, or huge messes in unexpected places?

Prince: I'll do anything else you want, but please let me keep them…I love them.

Queen: If you insist, here are the rules: you find the money to feed them; if they harm anyone, they go; and NO DRAGONS in my suite, the kitchen or the dining room.

Prince: Anything you say.

Tutor: The Prince was never happier. The dragons were always very obedient with their master. But I noticed something that he didn't. With other people…those creatures would be restless, a little wild, as was their true nature.

Shadow of Dragons

Prince: Watch this: lie down, good, now sit, good, now beg…wings out, that's it.

Gives them treat.

Have you ever seen such a beautiful sight? Here, you try now.

Tutor: Never seen anything like it.

Prince: You make them follow like this…heel.

Tutor: Oh, yes, just like that.

Commoner 1: Will you look at that. See how far spoiling a child can go?

Commoner 2: The beasts are outside, coming this way!

Commoner 1: Shut the door.

Commoner 2: Close the shutters.

Commoner 1: He's a strange one…delivered same night as a cat and goat, I hear.

Commoner 2: What with no father, a weak mother, poor kid.

Commoner 1: Poor kid, indeed!

Commoner 2:	He's harnessing them, he's taught them to fly, he's riding them.
Commoner 1:	Look at that bridle, the price of that bridle alone would buy me...
Commoner 2:	Those huge wings...
Commoner 1:	If he wants to ride, why not ride one of his Mother's prize thoroughbreds?
Commoner 2:	Not him, he wants flying monsters. Lord save us if he ever becomes King.
Commoner 1:	He won't live long enough to see the day. Rumour has it that one of the monsters nipped at the chamber maid, she quit then and there.

A COURTING HE SHOULD GO

Queen:	Tuto, where's that son of mine? Late again.
Tutor:	Look over there, he's arriving now.

Dragon flights can be gigantic shadows on rear wall.

Queen:	He's flying so low he's terrifying the workers. I've found something to take his mind off this childish obsession with monsters. Time he grew up.
Tutor:	There's something majestic about them in midair with their necks held high...and they follow his every command.
Queen:	Yes, it's time he follows that calling of a prince.
Tutor:	He's a good boy, really.
Queen:	*(enter Prince)* Glad you are finally here, safe and sound.
Prince:	I'm sorry, Mother, I did my best to hurry back.
Queen:	Well, now that we are assembled here, we need to discuss an important matter. You have come to a time in you're life where the stream and river meet and where the importance of one's goals becomes evident in the turbulent eddy of the ocean of life. It is then that we realize that our responsibilities are an awesome task in light of...
Prince:	What are you trying to say?
Queen:	To put it plainly, it's time you married.
Prince:	Married.
Queen:	Think about it: I'm not getting any younger, there's much to

	hand over to you before I go on to the next life. And I'm quite ready for some grandchildren.
Prince:	Grandchildren.
Queen:	Yes, we can find you a pretty young princess in a neighbouring country and have a grand wedding. I remember Germany's daughter as a strong, lovely young woman, the deepest blue eyes...or maybe you have some other princess in mind?
Prince:	I haven't really thought about it.
Queen:	And there's the daughter of France, she does beautiful embroidery, remember?
Prince:	No.
Queen:	And Spain has several daughters to choose from. Where shall we start?
Prince:	You seem to know them well. You can choose for me. I have only one condition: if you want to arrange a marriage, I'll marry the girl who agrees to ride with me on the dragons.
Queen:	Oh, the Prince of Surprises again! These are princesses bred in royal courts – I doubt that they aspire to ride dragons! They're only nice to you. And did you notice those dragons are not pleasant to anyone other than you? I wouldn't trust them with your bride.
Prince:	That's the only condition I have for a future wife.
Queen:	Keep a cautious eye on your "pets." You do make life... interesting!

A HUNTING THEY DO GO

Polka Music. They dance together.

Ambassador:	The Prince of Italy asked me to meet with you.
Princess of Germany:	
	Yes, I speak not good Italian. But I can good wife.
Ambassador:	I understand that you love Italy, and you've always wanted to live there.
Germany:	Italy I love and make best home.
Ambassador:	And your hobby is tapestry weaving.
Germany:	I beg you take show of my work to Prince.

Gives weaving.

Ambassador: Very lovely, he'll appreciate your kind gift. There's just one other matter to discuss. You've heard that the Prince has two dragons. Just two.

Germany: Yaaaas?

Ambassador: He, in his own unique way – the Prince is a special person, very strong – has set one condition on his future wife.

Germany: Strong man I like, what condition is?

Ambassador: *(very nonchalant)* He wants his future wife to ride his dragons with him. Didn't I say unique?

Germany: What unique? What dragon – I hear right – dragon, big, scaly, ugly, dangerous flying monster, wife ride?

Ambassador: Yes, isn't that funny? The Prince is so droll.

Germany: *(yells in German, then)* Droll? Me no fool, riding dragons this Princess?

Ambassador: *(laughs)* I take it you're not "gung ho" on the idea.

Germany: You take right! And you no take this to fool Prince.

> *Takes back weaving. Stomps on his foot. Exits.*

Ambassador: These are the times that try men's souls. I'll have to try a different approach with France.

> *Minuet music. She enters.*

Your Highness, I represent the great and exotic Prince of Italy who sends you this gift of fine perfume to grace Your Loveliness. He would be thrilled if you would grace his court with your presence.

Princess of France:

> *(giggling, doing needlework)* How charming. Je t'adore.

> *Flirting.*

Qu'est ce que vous voulez?

> *They dance.*

Ambassador: If you would consent to be his wife, you would have the greatest wedding that Europe has ever seen, and in keeping with his exotic tastes afterwards you would

> *Rushing this phrase.*

ride the incredible pet dragons.

France: Qu'est ce que la derriere phrase. "Le dragin?" Je ne connais pas "le dragin."

Ambassador: Oh, just a teensy ride on his pet dragon.

France: Dragon? Is she the giant flying animal with fire breath, she is dangerous ne'est ce pas?

Ambassador: No, they're pets really – they haven't killed anyone.

France: Mon dieu, I am not mad. I'm a noble princess, not a monster driver. Aurevoir au le fou prince!

Ambassador: I'm not getting very far. Off to the court of Spain. Can you imagine setting a marriage condition like that. He'll die a bachelor. Well, I can think of worse jobs, it's a living.

> *Enter Princess. She takes the lead right away. Spanish Tango music. They dance.*

Ambassador: *(lost confidence, expects to be rejected.)* Your Ladyship, the Prince of Italy would like you to consider an offer of marriage from him.

Princess of Spain:

I've heard about this Prince, they're rejecting him all over Europe.

Ambassador: Not exactly, it's not him they're rejecting...it's a conditional clause he has. He's a great person, loves archery, the mountains and the outdoors. And then there's his dragons.

Spain: I'm interested in these pets.

Ambassador: I know it sounds strange.

Spain: I never said that.

Ambassador: Every other one has said that.

Spain: I'm not every other one. Tell me about them.

Ambassador: *(very cautiously)* Well, he has two of them...they're trained...he rides them...and he wants his bride to ride the dragons with him, nuptial flight as it were.

Spain: Imagine soaring over buildings and towns, looking down on everyone like a bird, it must be wonderful.

Ambassador: You like the idea?

Spain: I'd consider it an honour. I can hardly wait. I could be offended that you didn't come here first, but then, the best is always saved until the last – isn't that right?

Ambassador: Oh, yes, I'm sorry I didn't come here first. You're certain about this? You want to marry the Prince, and you would LIKE to ride the dragons with him? Right?

Spain: Right!

Ambassador: Right.

Commoner 1:   And instead of a horse and carriage…"Climb onto my dragon, my dear…"

Commoner 2:   I wonder what kind of girl would have him. She must either be blind or stupid or both!

                Mock falsetto.

                "What's that, dear Prince? Where's the wagon I'm to get into? Oh my, this wagon is lifting off the ground. Oh, oh, dear me."

Commoner 1:   No, I think that she's just very smart. Some girls will do anything for money.

Commoner 2:   Well, you have a point. Money can't buy love, but it sure can make a person more likable.

ON THE BALCONY

Commoner 1:   I've been standing out here for hours to get a good spot, I want to see them real good.

Commoner 2:   Me, too, I've waited a long time to see a big royal wedding.

Commoner 3:   It's a fairy tale come true.

Commoner 4:   It's a rise in our taxes to pay for the whole darn thing is what it is.

Commoner 3:   But it's worth every penny, we need higher events to look up to, to inspire us.

Commoner 4:   You're better off aspiring to cook me some better meals so I've got the strength to work.

Commoner 3:   He's got no romance left in him.

                Bells, fanfare, confetti. Sound of crowd swells.

Commoner 2:   Oh, no! It's the big moment, I'm going to faint.

Commoner 4:   Good lord, she stands out here for 12 hours waiting for them to come out, and she misses the whole thing – unconscious!

Commoner 1:   The Princess doesn't look crazy. Imagine agreeing to ride dragons?

Commoner 2:   You can't tell if someone's crazy by just looking at them, although her *eyes* are set a bit close together, don't you think?

Commoner 3:	They're taking out the champagne glasses!
Commoner 4:	There go the taxes again, and I'm sure its not the cheap brand.
Commoner 3:	They're going to kiss!
Commoner 5:	Oh, yuck, slobber, bleah…
Commoner 3:	Now the Father of the bride has to kiss the Mother of the groom. Pass me a handkerchief.
Commoner 2:	It's too much, I can't stand it.
Commoner 4:	Neither can I.
Commoner 3:	He seems to have grown awfully gentle, not at all the wild young prince.
Commoner 2:	You know what they say, it takes marriage to settle a man down.
Commoner 4:	Don't I know it.
Crowd:	*(cheers)* Long live the Prince. Long live the Princess.
Commoner 1:	What's that?
	Projected shadows of dragons rise behind the couple.
Commoner 2:	It's his dragons.
Commoner 3:	It *was* so lovely, but he has to bring *them* out.
Commoner 4:	Let's get out of here.
	Scramble, then hushed quiet.

HONEYMOON FLIGHT

(In the first production, this flight was choreographed using two boards on a sawhorse with actors moving them up and down.)

Princess:	It takes my breath away. Look at the patchwork fields.
Prince:	Now you know why I like it.
Princess:	Those men down there are small as ants, they're running scared, they're afraid of us. They don't know what they're missing.
Prince:	I like this gentle gliding.
Princess:	And the floating in this huge sky. He's looking at me very strangely.
Prince:	I pulled left, come on now, turn!
Princess:	What is it?

Prince:	I don't know what's wrong, they're slower to follow than usual. We'll be back home soon, they'll get back to normal routine.
Princess:	She's twisting her head, sniffing, won't obey, what should I do?
Prince:	Easy now, behave, here's a treat...
Princess:	He almost snapped your hand off, they're ravenous. I don't like that.
Prince:	I fed them just before we left.

Dragons circle each other.

What is this? They've never done this before. A new trick to impress my wife?

Prince struggles to control them, both dragons hiss, snort and slowly become wilder.

Princess:	She's stopped in midair, won't move. They look vicious.
Prince:	Put those tongues back in your heads or I'll cut them off. Biting, too! You beasts, take this!
Princess:	*(dragons try to throw them off)* Help, I'm losing my balance. It's hard to control her. Ouch, I'm hurt.
Prince:	We'll land. Keep trying to get them to land.

Dragons circle each other snapping at riders.

Prince:	We're close enough to the ground—jump off, quick!

They both jump and are now on guard against the enemy.

Princess:	They've turned wild.

Dragon shadows return on screen/wall.

Prince:	I'll tame them!

Shoots.

Princess:	It's made them madder. They're coming at us.

Shoots again. Dragons wounded. Still stalking.

Prince:	I'll finish them off for good.

Shoots and kills. Writhing and last gasps of dragons.

Princess:	How can we be sure they're dead?
Prince:	They're dead. I remember seeing other dead dragons long ago, and they looked just like this. I thought they would grow up differently. They were treated well. I raised them from

helpless babies to trusted companions. I never imagined …what if…how can they turn…oh, it's over now.

Princess: We can't see into creatures' hearts, you couldn't know.

Prince: I'm still shaking at what might have been. I have to say good-bye to them. I don't understand. It's sad, but we're all right. Good-bye.

Princess: We've got some daylight left, let's cover as much distance as we can towards the setting sun.

Mime: Across stream, up hills, through bush, tired, running down. Exhausted.

Princess: Fresh water.

Prince: Let's stop here.

Falls asleep.

AT THE PALACE

Queen: It's now three days, no sign of them.

Tutor: The search party has gone over the same land twice.

Queen: They can't have disappeared into thin air.

Tutor: They've probably taken a side trip. The Princess was so taken with flying that they may have ventured into France. A little holiday.

Queen: I feel it in my bones that something's not right.

Tutor: They're bright young people, they can look after themselves.

Queen: It's easy for you to say, it's not your child. I'm sorry Tuto, I didn't mean it. I'm terrified.

Tutor: We'll send the searchers out one more time. Spain is also covering his territory, it takes time to get messengers back and forth.

Queen: You do that.

She prays.

The woods. A dark night. Weak with hunger.

Prince: I think we're close, I remember this part of the woods.

Princess: I hope so, I don't know how much longer we can go on.

Rustling.

What's that?

Prince: Hide, quick.

Gets bow ready.

Here.

Princess: No, it's a person.

Prince: I'm so happy to see you.

Tutor: And who are you?

Prince: You know me. My bow and arrow.

Tutor: The archer makes those by the dozen.

Prince: Who's got a wart on his right pinkie?

Tutor: Ah, there was a wart epidemic a few years ago. Don't waste my time. I'm looking for the Prince of Italy who's disappeared on his way back from Spain. Have you seen him and his bride? They were riding the dragons last time we saw them. The Queen's in a black mood, it's terrible.

Prince: Tuto, look at me very carefully.

Tutor: I see two tattered wanderers.

Prince: What can I say…

Looks around.

Ah! A wild rose, species *Rosa Acicularis Lindl,* the Wild Rose. We dug this out of the garden because Mother wanted only domesticated roses.

Tutor: Is it really you? Of course, look at your eyes. God bless you, aren't you glad you learned your lessons? The Princess? Thank God, our prayers are answered. What happened? Where's the dragons? Here's some food and drink. You poor things.

Prince: It's a strange and heartbreaking story, I'll tell you while we move toward home.

HOMECOMING

Tutor: Hello, open up.

Queen: *(has put a black veil on her head)* Go away you drunkard, if you'd lost a son, you'd be mourning.

Tutor: It's me, Your Majesty. I have good news.

Queen: Ah, yes, my faithful servant, who has followed my poor son through all his growing up. You've seen him through so much. Why did we let him take so many chances? What should we

	have done?
Tutor:	She's been ranting for days, no one can do anything for her. Your Highness, rejoice, your prayers are answered.
Queen:	Go away until you return with my son, not with beggars or rogues.
Tutor:	Look again, it's...
Queen:	No use discussing it. I'll keep a vigil here until he's found.
Tutor:	He is found.
Queen:	Found where?
Tutor:	Here.
Queen:	Here?
Prince:	Here.
Queen:	Oh, my dear, why didn't you say so? And your family is sick with worry. We'll send a messenger right away. What happened? Where are the dragons?
Princess:	It's still hard to think about. They're dead. Like those dragons long ago on the summit. I guess it wasn't meant to be.
Queen:	You did what you had to do.
Tutor:	You're back safely. And I'd love to show you the ground. We can show you the only eagle's nest in a garden in this area.
Princess:	An eagle's nest? In Arabia the Kings and their tribesmen tame falcons. Maybe we could tame your eagles?
Prince:	Tame the eagles?
Tutor:	I've heard the question before around here...long ago, before we had dragons...
Queen:	You must be exhausted, save that for later.
Tutor:	Birds of a feather...
Queen:	Flock together?

The End

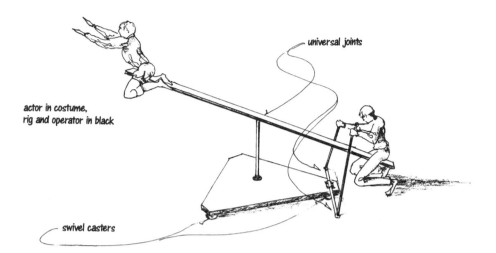

universal joints

actor in costume,
rig and operator in black

swivel casters

The Old Woman and the Pedlar

BETTY JANE WYLIE

Design Concept by Tara Ryan

BETTY JANE WYLIE is an author of an eclectic range of stage and radio plays, poetry, operas, essays, children's literature and adult nonfiction. She has received an Icelandic-Canadian Poetry Prize and an Education Award from the Ontario Psychological Association. Betty Jane Wylie is an active member of the Writers Union of Canada, which she served as chairperson during 1988-89. She has been Writer in Residence at the Burlington Public Library, Burlington, Ontario, and she was a member of the Banff Centre's Playwrights Colony during the summer of 1989.

The Old Woman and the Pedlar was first produced by Young People's Theatre, Toronto, Ontario, in September, 1977, with the following cast playing the different characters interchangeably:

Jennifer Browne
Bonnie Green
Don Richie
Christopher Youngren

Directed by Joyce Doolittle
Designed by Michael Maher
Original Music by Quenten Doolittle

CHARACTERS
The Old Woman
The Mute
The Pedlar/Total ReCall/Super Sam, the Space Salesman
Dr. Noodle/Hope, the Dream Merchant

PLAYWRIGHT'S NOTE
Based on the nursery rhyme, "Lawk-a-mercy On Me," *The Old Woman and the Pedlar* is a play about the search for identity, but it is a playful search. The Old Woman falls asleep by the side of the road and a Pedlar cuts off her skirts. "Lawk-a-mercy on me," she cries when she wakes up shivering, "This is none of I!" Even her dog, Winston, doesn't know her, so she has to find out who she is. A number of characters help her in the search, and the emphasis is on play – word-play and play-acting, games and puzzles and slapstick and charming confrontations with a crazy doctor, a space salesman, a name-dropper, a dream merchant, a silent boy and, of course, the Pedlar. There is much mime and much use of charades because the silent boy is mute. There is one song based on the nursery rhyme.

The Old Woman and the Pedlar

The cast sings the introductory song.

There was a little woman as I've heard tell.
Lawk-a-mercy, this is none of I.
She went to market her eggs for to sell.
Lawk-a-mercy, this is none of I.
She went to market all on a market day,
And she fell asleep on the King's Highway.
Lawk-a-mercy, lawk-a-mercy,
Hey nonny nonny, this is none of I.
Along came a pedlar, his name was Stout.
Lawk-a-mercy, this is none of I.
He cut her petticoats all round about.
Lawk-a-mercy, this is none of I.
He cut her petticoats up to her knees,
Which made the old woman to shiver and sneeze.
Lawk-a-mercy, lawk-a-mercy,
Hey nonny nonny, this is none of I.
When this little woman first did awake,
Lawk-a-mercy, this is none of I.
She began to shiver and began to shake.
Lawk-a-mercy, this is none of I.
And she began to wonder and began to cry.
Oh, lawk-a-mercy me, this is none of I.

a regular, school flip-type easel or, if enough people are available,

a sandwich board

Lights up on an empty stage. Signpost with 'Market' pointing one way, 'Home' pointing the other way. A Pedlar with a pack enters.

can be anchored in a pot of sand or hung or nailed to a board painted like grass

Pedlar: Hello. I'm a pedlar, and this is my pack. I have everything – I mean everything, in my pack – past, present and future. Oh, yes, I buy people's pasts and sometimes their futures. But I steal their presents. If they don't look after their presents, they deserve to lose them. Time is very precious, especially present-time. I mean right now. Where would you be if you didn't have right now? You wouldn't be here. You have to have now to be here. So, hang onto your now, or I'll take it!

Laughs.

And I won't give it back! I'll sell it.

Enter the Old Woman hustling by on her way

Pedlar

a vest with many pockets

Use either bold and bright – almost hippish or fantastic – colours or perhaps try a neutral, secondhand shop look (ie. old tails and vest) pack options:
almost any very large, easily removed knapsack – it should look old and well used – or any large handbag with lots of travel stamps

also try to reflect a magician in the costume if possible

Old Woman
possible options:

kerchief and rollers, hornrim glasses, apron, fuzzy pink slippers
use bright, tacky colours and create a sort of nightmare modern housewife

bun, shawl, Saralee apron, boots, should be tattered up and layered
the style and colour of the old womans outfit should reflect how you want the audience to feel about her: eg. sad, foolish, etc.
she should have a purse or money pouch

perhaps have some pots and spoons attached to the pedlar's pack or vest

magic scarf can be found at most hobby shops

sparkle spray is also available at most hobby shops

home from market. She doesn't speak to the Pedlar as she goes by, so he speaks to her.

Pedlar: How do you do, and how do you do, and how do you do again?

Old Woman: Well, and well, and well, I thank you. I've been to market and sold all my eggs, and I'm on my way home as fast as my legs can carry me.

Pedlar: Slow down, stop a bit, hold on a little, let me show you what's in my pack. I've magic for sale, and dreams and fantasy and something for your kitchen, too.

Old Woman: I can't stop. My dog, Winston, is waiting for me at home, and I have so much work…

He aims his cane at her and she is pulled back by magic.

What kind of magic?

Pedlar: Tailor-made, trimmed to fit, any colour you choose.

He takes a silk scarf from his pack, pulls it through his hand and it changes colour.

Old Woman: And dreams, you say…mine are getting a bit tarnished.

Pedlar: Buy some of my polish then…

He whips out a spray can and sprays a circle in the air.

guaranteed to put the sparkle back in your dreams. Nonstick, self-polishing, complete satisfaction or your money back. How are you fixed for fantasy?

Old Woman: It doesn't last the way it used to. My fantasy is threadbare and barely covers my eyes. I can see right through it.

Pedlar: *(hard sell)* What you need is a Magic Mender. Magic Mender!! It pleats, smocks, stitches, darns or mends all in one silent operation. Restores any fantasy or dream in minutes. Guaranteed for six months or sixty thousand stitches, which ever comes first. Just lock in place and stitch away. Click! It's locked; just crank away. That's all there is to it. Only $7.95 for the gadget of the century! Of course, the thread comes extra.

Dream Machine

an abacus with colourful thread woven through it or something with a crank – maybe a meat grinder

Old Woman: Thread?

Pedlar: You can't expect to reinforce a fantasy or darn a dream without thread, can you? Darn-a-Dream thread is high quality gossamer – none of your thick homespun make-believe stuff. Comes in all colours of the rainbow plus silver, gold and star blush.

Old Woman: Star blush? What's that?

Pedlar: It's a colour that was discontinued years ago. However, I've been in the business for years. My pack is very old. You wouldn't believe what's in my pack.

He rummages in his pack.

I know I still have that Star Blush here somewhere. Come now, shall I find it for you? To go with your Darn-a-Dream Kit?

Old Woman: No...no...no! I don't know why I bother talking to you. I don't need your fix-it kits.

She starts away again, and he uses the cane to draw her back.

I don't dream any more.

Pedlar: That's exactly why you do need them.

Old Woman: No. I have a very short memory. Yesterday is gone, and tomorrow is far off. Now is enough for me.

Pedlar: Are you sure?

Old Woman: Quite sure.

Pedlar: Then you'd better hang on to it.

Old Woman: What?

She shakes her head at him as if to ward off an annoying fly.

Right now, I have to get home to my dog, Winston, with my egg money before my legs fall off. I've been walking all day, and I'm almost ready to drop. I'm off. Good day to you, until the next time.

Pedlar: If there is a next time. You take too much for granted. You

*either huge garden shears
or cardboard fakes*

before

velcro

*panel
skirt*

after

slip

*using velcro to attach the
skirt makes it reusable and
the sound of the velcro
detaching sounds like tearing*

*underneath perhaps she is
wearing torn hose, men's
boxer shorts, long johns or
men's sock garters*

think now is going to last forever. I wouldn't count on it if I were you.

Old Woman: But I'm not.

Pedlar: Not what?

Old Woman: Not you.

Pedlar: Are you sure?

Old Woman: Not very.

Pedlar: Well, don't count on it, then. You shouldn't count your eggs before they're hatched.

Old Woman: I never do.

Pedlar: Or on your legs before they're home.

The Pedlar exits. The Old Woman walks on but slower and finally stops.

Old Woman: My legs are ready to fall off! Oh, lawk-a-mercy on me! I have to sit down…and lie down…and sleep…

She falls asleep. The Pedlar comes back.

Pedlar: Ah, hah! What did I tell you? Her legs didn't carry her home. It just goes to show – you shouldn't count on anything. Don't believe anything you hear and only half of what you see. Now, I am going to teach her a lesson. She wouldn't buy my Darn-a-Dream Thread and my Magic Mender. Well, we'll see who needs a Magic Mender now…

He whips scissors out of his pack and cuts off her skirt just above her knee. He stuffs the bottom of her skirt into his pack.

I'll just keep her skirt in my pack.

To the Old Woman.

Now, you're going to be cold, and you're going to shiver and shake until you awake…

He laughs and exits.

Old woman: Oh, I'm cold! I'm shaking to pieces I'm so cold! My legs feel like blocks of ice.

She looks down at her legs and screams.

My legs, my legs! No wonder my legs are cold. My skirt is gone! This can't be me. It's not me. I have stopped being me. I must be somebody else with a short skirt. But…it feels like me. The rest of me seems the same. And here's my egg basket…and my egg money. But it's not me.

If this be I and I hope it be,
I have a little dog at home and he knows me;
If it be I he'll wag his little tail,
And if it be not I he'll loudly bark and wail.

> *She starts offstage in the direction of home. Offstage, as she disappears from view, we hear the dog set up a terrible racket. She runs back on stage.*

My dog Winston never barks at me. Therefore…I can't be me. Well, then…since I am not me, I must be someone else. I'll have to find out who I am.

> *Enter the Mute. He can be sweeping or juggling balls or simply enjoying life – whatever appeals to the actor.*

Oh sir, oh sir, you're just the person I've been looking for.

> *The Mute looks around to make sure she's not talking to someone else. He does a 'who, me?' gesture.*

Yes, you. Yes, I've been waiting for you to come along, to tell me who I am. Tell me, who am I?

> *The Mute shrugs, but she hardly notices, she's so busy talking.*

Do I look different to you?

> *He notices her missing skirt and tries to hide his laughter so as not to hurt her feelings.*

I feel different. My dog thinks I'm different. Am I different? Do I look like the egg lady who goes to the market on Saturdays? Tell me!

Dog
options:
bring puppet dog on stage or have an actor play a live dog

since it is usually more interesting if action occurs on the stage, perhaps she could be chased up the tree

Mute
options:
a mime – in black with white gloves and a white face, a bum or hobo in rags, a clown, or maybe a salesclerk on a lunch break

mime mute should be wearing suspenders with various kinds of noisemakers around the neck

> *The Mute shrugs again. But suddenly he has a thought. He holds up a hand to tell her.*

You've thought of something?

> *He nods. He holds up six fingers.*

Six fingers?

> *He shakes his head.*

Charades! It's a game! You're going to show me six words!

> *He nods and holds up one finger.*

First word...

> *They do a charade together to find the proverb "A stitch in time saves nine."*

A stitch in time saves nine!

> *The Old Woman is delighted with herself for having solved the charade, then remembers her problems and can't see what good this is doing her.*

Nine what?

> *The Mute shrugs.*

What does it matter, nine what? That still doesn't tell me who I am.

> *The Mute shrugs his sympathy and makes a good-bye gesture.*

Oh, yes – good-bye. Thanks, anyway.

> *The Mute exits.*

A stitch in time saves nine...stitch, stitch...maybe I'm not an egg lady. Maybe I'm a dressmaker. A stitch in time saves nine – nine what? A stitch ane tame saves nane. O stoatch oan tome soves none. Ee steetch een teeme seeves neene...

> *She is interrupted by the Mute coming back onstage leading Dr. Noodle. She is wearing a white coat and has a giant stethoscope around her neck. She is accompanied by the Mute, who carries her doctor's bag for her.*

Noodle: How are you, how are you? And how are we today?

Old Woman: Fine, fine, just fine.

Noodle: Now, what seems to be the trouble? I'm Dr. Noodle, here to help you.

Old Woman: Oh, I need you, Dr. Noodle. I'm not well. I'm not well at all.

Dr. Noodle whips up the stethoscope and places it on the Old Woman's chest.

Doctor

Noodle: I knew it, I knew it! I knew it the minute I laid eyes on you. I'm never wrong. I knew there was something the matter with you. Noodle, I said to myself, that woman needs Noodle, or my name's not Noodle. And it is.

Old Woman: Is what?

Noodle: Noodle. Hark!

doctor's bag

As she listens on her stethoscope, we hear the peculiar thumping of the Old Woman's heart – perhaps the tune of the song.

Mmmm! That's a very interesting heartbeat you have here.

could be a cheap shopping bag or

The Mute listens in on one earpiece, too, and the two do a little jig in time to the beat.

Very interesting. Boy! My bag, if you please.

The Mute opens her bag and holds it out. She picks up a long scarf and pokes it in the Old Woman's ear. The Mute pulls it out the other ear. Noodle examines the scarf.

a bag full of all sorts of funny/scary found-at-home implements or

Clean as a whistle – nothing there to worry about. What seems to be the trouble, exactly?

Noodle picks up a tongue depressor, and as the Old Woman starts to answer the question she pokes it in her mouth so that the words are garbled and incomprehensible. But she is trying to say, "My skirt is gone and my dog barked at me and I don't know who I am."

a supply cart pushed by the mime/mute; doctor can ride on it like a queen

if the centre section of the set includes moveable boxes, the mute may be able to arrange them chair-like to accommodate the examination or maybe use the cart as a place for the examination

Speak up, speak up! How do you expect anyone to understand you if you don't enunciate clearly? Mmm – your throat looks a little raw there. Let's just have another peek. Now, tell me, what's your trouble?

She puts the tongue depressor in again.

Old Woman: *(garbled)* I fell asleep and my skirt disappeared and my dog didn't know me

extra-large glasses for smart look for assistant exaggerate prop size

and if he doesn't, who does?

Noodle: I can't understand a word you're saying. Do try to make yourself clear. Open wide…

> *She puts the depressor in again. The Old Woman shouts frantically around it. The first two words, "I've lost" are shouted clearly but the rest is garbled.*

You shouldn't shout so. No wonder your throat is so raw-looking. You'd better gargle some baking soda and hot water before you go to bed tonight.

> *To the Mute.*

Write that down, boy! Lost something, have you?

Old Woman: My skirt.

Noodle: I knew there was something strange about you! I said that, didn't I, boy? I said, "There's something strange about that woman. Something's the matter there." Where did you lose your skirt?

Old Woman: Right here.

Noodle: *(looking around)* Where is it, then?

Old Woman: If I knew that, it wouldn't be lost. It disappeared while I was asleep. I woke up because I was cold.

Noodle: Ah, hah! That's where you got your sore throat! Write that down, boy.

Old Woman: And I went home and my dog didn't know me and he barked at me and I got very upset and…

Noodle: Upset? You mustn't get upset. That's very hard on the blood pressure.

> *Noodle hauls out a blood pressure kit from the bag, the circus kind, using a bicycle pump. She wraps the cloth around the Old Woman's arm.*

use some type of balloon
attached to the pump

Old Woman: I got very…

Noodle: Go on, go on with what you're saying. I'm listening, I'm not missing a word. Are you writing it all down, boy?

> *The Mute nods and keeps on writing, but he has to stop to help pump.*

Old Woman: I got very upset and I came back here and I'm trying to find out who I am. First, a noisy little boy came along and he wouldn't stop talking – I could hardly hear myself think he talked so much and then I played games with him and I don't know what a stitch in time saves and...

> *A large balloon has been growing out of the wrapping on the Old Woman's arm. It gets bigger and bigger until it explodes – use a pin. The Old Woman yells, falls backward and Noodle and the Mute pick her up.*

Noodle: Just as I thought. You're suffering from extremely high blood pressure. You mustn't get so excited. Keep calm. Calm, calm, calm, calm, calm. Isn't that what I always say? Are you writing this down, boy? Now, just let me have your name and medical insurance number and I'll be on my way.

Old Woman: I don't know my name. I thought I knew who I was but I don't any more.

Noodle: Not know your own name! Why that's terrible! You must be really sick!

Old Woman: You're the doctor. You're supposed to make me better.

having the mute begin to pull out yards of red tape (ribbon maybe) makes the following lines literal

Noodle: I'm not equipped to do nominations. That's a job for a specialist. Oh, well, just give me your address and number and we'll let someone else worry about it. That's what red tape is for. Address?

Old Woman: I don't live there any more.

Noodle: Where?

Old Woman: Where my dog lives. Winston barked at me so I can't live there any more. I guess I don't live anywhere.

Noodle: Nonsense! Everyone lives somewhere. Anyone with half an eye can see you're living right there, right in front of me.

Old Woman: Oh, I'm alive and well, but living where I don't know.

Noodle: Boy, tear up the notes. I can't do a thing for her.

The Mute tears up his paper and tosses the scraps in the air.
Then he sees the mess he has made, gets his broom and sweeps it
up. Dr. Noodle shuts her bag and leaves. The Mute follows.

Old Woman:	The farther I go, the less I know. If I don't even know my own name, how can I expect anyone else to remember anything about me. Oh, if only I could remember!

Enter Total Recall.

ReCall:	I'm just the person you're looking for, then.
Old Woman:	Who are you?
ReCall:	Total ReCall is my name.
Old Woman:	What do you do?
ReCall:	I'm a name-dropper. I drop names at the drop of a hat.
Old Woman:	If you dropped my name do you think I could pick it up again?
ReCall:	No doubt about it. I bring up names, too. The heavier the better. Listen to this one: Fats McGoogle. He's one of the heaviest names I know. Like it?
Old Woman:	Do I have to?
ReCall:	Not at all, not at all. I was just giving you a free sample, that's all.
Old Woman:	Oh, do you usually charge?
ReCall:	Not always. It depends. It's not nice to be too free with names, you know, especially other people's names. A name is a person's most precious possession. Once lost it's hard to recover, especially a good one.
Old Woman:	Oh, dear. Oh, dear.
ReCall:	Why, what's wrong?
Old Woman:	I wish you hadn't said that.
ReCall:	What did I say?
Old Woman:	You said once a name is lost it's hard to recover.
ReCall:	That's true, it is. What's so terrible about saying that?
Old Woman:	I've lost my name.
ReCall:	Oh, that is too bad. However did it happen?
Old Woman:	Well, I fell asleep by the side of the road and when I woke up my skirt was gone and my dog didn't know me, which proved it

wasn't I, so now I don't know who I am.

ReCall:	Maybe I can help you. I'm very good at names.
Old Woman:	Oh, I'd be so grateful if you could.
ReCall:	Well, I'll try. Now – let's see. Was it a male or a female name?
Old Woman:	Female, I think.
ReCall:	Was it a long or short name?
Old Woman:	Long, I think. I can remember my Father saying he never trusted anyone who only had one syllable to his name.
ReCall:	So…two or three syllable female names. Well, now, I'll just drop a few and you stop me if you hear one you'd like to pick up: Abigail, Beatrice, Clematis, Kimberly, Leila, Mary Jane, Nuala, Orchid, Peony, Quinella, Rosalee, Yolande, Zorah…there! Did any of those sound like you?
Old Woman:	No…no, I don't think so. That was lovely, though.
ReCall:	Thank you. I thought it was rather well done myself. Well, dear, I guess you'll just have to get on with it.
Old Woman:	On with what?
ReCall:	You're going to have to make a name for yourself. You may pick one up faster than most.
Old Woman:	Why is that?
ReCall:	Because you look pretty funny in that short skirt. People are going to start calling you names! Cheerio!
	He exits.
Old Woman:	Cheerio? Nothing's very cheery to me now. I've lost my shirt. I've lost my dog. I've lost my name. And now I'm losing my hope.
	Music.
Hope:	*(from offstage)* Someone calling me?

Recall

could be a bookworm or

a card dealer

Recall could have a sachel (paperboy's sack) full of scrolls
names would be located on scrolls (possibly window blinds)
names could be performed to a tune with either the mute performing the music or the audience clapping and stamping in rhythm

<table>
<tr><td>Old Woman:</td><td>Not consciously.</td></tr>
</table>

Hope enters carrying balloons, dancing to the music theme.

Who are you?

Hope

Hope:	My name is Hope and I'm a Dream Merchant. Did I hear you say you were losing your hope? Hope is never lost. I've never been lost a day in my life. I may have been dashed and given up and even abandoned, but very few people lose me, not all of me. I spring eternal. I thought everyone knew that.
Old Woman:	Well, yes, I had heard something like that about you. But I don't think there's a thing you can do for me.

Hope as a child
barefoot with pockets full of
things to blow bubbles with

Hope:	Try me. Just look at these dreams of mine. I have dreams to suit every fancy. Look, look! Dreams of glory, dreams of yesteryear, daydreams, pipe dreams, dream houses and castles and boats, not to mention visions and illusions, fantasies and fond hopes. There must be something here for you. What's your trouble?
Old Woman:	You see, I thought I knew who I was and where I was going.
Hope:	Who were you and where were you going?

Hope as a singing messenger

Old Woman:	I was the egg lady, and I was going to market to sell my eggs. And then I was coming home from market with my egg money, but I fell asleep by the side of the road, and when I woke up my skirt was gone, my dog didn't know me and neither did I. I've lost my home, my name and now I'm losing all hope.
Hope:	No, no. Not all hope. I'm still here, and I wouldn't dream of leaving you.
Old Woman:	Well, that's very nice of you but...who am I?
Hope:	Who would you like to be?
Old Woman:	Oh...oh...oh...I never thought of that.

Hope: Well, think about it. That's the most important thing of all. How can you find yourself if you don't know who it is you want to find?

Old Woman: I never thought of it that way.

Hope: Do you really want to be who you used to be? Here, I'll give you a dream of yesteryear and see how you like it...

Hope hands a helium-filled balloon to the Old Woman, but it slips from her grasp and floats up to the ceiling. She watches it disappear.

Hope: I can see you didn't want to hang on to that dream.

Here's a dream of glory...

As soon as the Old Woman touches it, it fizzles out and onto the floor.

That went flat, didn't it? Well, here's a daydream...

The daydream balloon – filled with 2 tablespoons of water – falls splat to the floor.

That's the trouble with daydreams – they just lie there. The only way they're ever going to work is if people decide to make them come true. We'll have to try a pipe dream, then, though I must warn you, they're even more undependable than daydreams.

Music. Hope whips out a pipe-wand and a bottle of magic bubble solution and blows a few bubbles for the Old Woman. The Old Woman reaches for them ,but they burst when she touches them.

You see what I mean? No tensile strength at all. I don't think you want a dream house or a castle or a boat. No, I think the best thing for you after all is a fond hope. Give me your hand.

Music again. The Old Woman gives Hope her hand. Hope turns her hand over, plants a kiss in the palm and then closes the Old Woman's fingers over it.

There! Hang on to that. You'll be all right. You'll see...

Hope leaves, taking her balloons with her.

Old Woman: Thank you, Hope. Thank you very much.

Sighs.

I feel better. Things are going to be all right. I have a fond hope. I'm going to find out who I want to be, and then I'll know how to find out who I am.

Pause.

I have to think about that. I should make a little list. What I really need now is some paper.

Super Sam enters with a large blank drawing pad on an easel and a big Magic Marker felt pen.

if easel is used throughout the play to simulate location change, then Sam could just pick it up on his way onto the stage
have more than one colour of marker

Sam: And that's exactly what I have for you today. Paper! All that lovely, empty space, just waiting to be filled!

Sam

a french artist or...

Old Woman: Who are you?

Sam: I'm Super Sam, the Space Salesman.

Old Woman: What kind of space do you sell?

Sam: You name it, I've got it – for a price. I sell all kinds of space: inner space, outer space, blank space, narrow space, open space, cupboard space. No one can ever get enough cupboard space.

Old Woman: I could use some more cupboard space.

the tacky fast-talking greasy-looking car salesman with slicked-back hair, loud tie, pinky rings, white shoes, three-piece matching polyester tweed-look suit, gold-embossed briefcase for contracts

Sam: I thought I heard you say you wanted paper. That's what I brought you – empty space.

Old Woman: Oh, yes, that's right. I thought if I made a little list, I might find out who I wanted to be and then I might find out who I am and then I might find out where I'm going.

Sam: Oh, you do have a problem!

Old Woman: I know that.

Sam: Paper isn't going to solve your problem. I can't solve your problem. You're going to have to solve your problem all by yourself.

Old Woman: Yes, but how? I don't know where to start.

Sam: Start right here.

Old Woman: Where?

Sam: Here.

Sam draws an X on the paper with the

Magic Marker.

Now get to work!

He hands her the Magic Marker and leaves.

Old Woman: No, wait! Don't go!

The Mute enters, sweeping.

Everyone keeps leaving me. I'm getting tired of this. Oh, I wish Winston were here!

Pause.

But Winston needs taking care of, too. I bet he's getting awfully hungry. Oh, dear! I must do something! But what?

Sam

a little league coach –
silky league jacket, baseball
cap, chewing gum or...

The Mute stops sweeping, takes the Magic Marker from her and with a flourish writes the number 7 on the paper and waits for her to respond.

Another charade?

The Mute nods.

Seven words?

The Mute nods again. Ad-lib as they work out the following: "Silence is golden, but whistles call dogs."

Repeats it once she has solved it.

Silence is golden, but whistles call dogs. That's very good, and true, too. Now, where can I find a whistle?

a far-out, space-type
creature – motorcycle
helmet, ping pong balls for
eyes, vacuum tubing and
other weird-looking things
attached to a set of
workman's overalls

The Mute stops her with a quick reminder: first the silence, then the whistle. The Old Woman repeats as she gets the clues and agrees.

First the silence...all right, I'm speechless.

The Mute gestures to a place for her to sit. He draws a flower on the paper, tears it off and crumples it up in his hand. He then waves his other hand over it and comes up with a bright flower, which he presents to the Old Woman. She is touched and starts to speak but remembers she must not and puts

a magic trick
mute crumples paper and
then pretends to pull flowers
from the wad (feather from
sleeve)

similar to a one-man band

her fingers over her lips in time. She accepts
the flower and smiles at him. She wants to
give him something and remembers her fond
hope. She raises her hand and beckons him
to come closer. He does. She opens her hand
slowly and blows her fond hope off her palm
towards him. He feels it touch his cheek,
puts his hand to the spot and smiles.

The Pedlar enters banging on a bucket.

Old Woman:	Stop that racket!

More noise.

Pedlar:	Why?

More noise.

Old Woman:	Because I am getting angry.
Pedlar:	Good! I was wondering if you ever would.

*The Old Woman stands up, turns on the
Pedlar and shakes her finger at him.*

Old Woman:	You! You're the one! I wouldn't be a bit surprised if it was you all along.
Pedlar:	Neither would I.
Old Woman:	You're the one who took my skirt, my dog and my name away from me. And now you're taking my silence and trying to steal my last fond hope! Well, I won't stand for it any more! I'm going to fight you!

the easel could be a part of
the puppet element or on
rollers

Pedlar:	What with?
Old Woman:	What with? With all of my might!

behind an exactly calculated
number of pieces of paper
there would be a box with a
drawer

Pedlar:	What else?

*The Old Woman goes to the easel and draws
a box with a door on it. She rips the paper
door open, opens a door behind it and pulls
out two wooden swords. She turns in
triumph to the Pedlar.*

Old Woman:	Choose your weapon!

The Pedlar hefts them and picks one.

Old Woman:	En garde!

use funny, exaggerated
swords

They fight – a punch-and-judy stick fight. Lots of noise, panting, etc. She finally overcomes him and knocks his sword out of his hands.

Ah, hah! Do you give up?

She tickles him and he laughs.

Pedlar: I give up.

Laughs again.

Old Woman: What's so funny?

Pedlar: I knew you could do it if you tried.

Old Woman: Do what?

Pedlar: Fight for what belongs to you.

Old Woman: *(very pleased with herself)* I did, didn't I? Well, where do we go from here? What do I do now?

Pedlar: Now, we call Winston.

Old Woman: How?

Pedlar: With a whistle, of course. You need a whistle to call your dog.

The Pedlar rummages in his pack and hands a drawstring bag to the Mute. The Mute tries several different whistles. The last one is effective ,and we hear Winston barking offstage. The Mute runs off and brings back Winston – either a puppet or a real dog. Winston jumps into the Old Woman's lap.

Old Woman: Winston! Am I ever glad to see you! And you know me now. I have a feeling that pretty soon I'll know me, too.

Pedlar: So you've got your dog back.

Old Woman: He's not mine. I'm his.

Pedlar: Quite right, quite right. What you need now is a Magic Mender. Boy, take Winston out for a bone.

The Mute takes Winston away.

I have a Magic Mender that...

Old Woman: Are you still trying to sell me that?

Pedlar: You really need it now. How else are you going to put your skirt back on?

Old Woman: But I've lost my skirt.

The Pedlar rummages in his pack.

Pedlar:	I'm sure I saw something…ah, here it is! Is this what you had in mind?

He holds up her cut-off skirt. The Old Woman gets angry again.

Old Woman:	That's the rest of my skirt! I knew it! You had it all along! Give me that!

But the Pedlar dodges her grasp and runs away. She runs after him, and there is a good chase with the usual slapstick routines.

Old Woman:	Oh, if I ever get my hands on you, I'll…
Pedlar:	You'll what?
Old Woman:	Get my skirt back.
Pedlar:	Try and catch me, then.

More chase.

Old Woman:	Stop! Stop!
Pedlar:	This morning you were the one who wouldn't stop. Now you want me to stop. Why?
Old Woman:	Because – I'm going to get you.

More chase.

Pedlar:	It isn't me you want to get; it's yourself.

The Pedlar sits centre stage while the Old Woman keeps on running, not noticing.

Are you having any fun?

Old Woman:	Yes! Yes, I am! I haven't had such a good run in years.

She stops.

Pedlar:	Good! Now you can have your skirt. But first, tell me what you've learned today. Remember what you said: yesterday is gone and tomorrow is far off; now is enough for me. Now, what do you say?
Old Woman:	I say…that I said the right things for the wrong reasons. Yesterday is gone and tomorrow is far off, but that's why now is so important and not to be rushed through. Now is where I am.
Pedlar:	Now you can have your skirt.

The Old Woman takes the skirt and is vainly trying to hold it onto the bottom edge of her remaining skirt.

Old Woman:	Oh, my skirt, my skirt! How am I ever going to get it back on?
Pedlar:	I told you you'd need my Magic Mender sooner or later.
	Goes into his Barker's Spiel.
	Magic Mender! It pleats, smocks…
Old Woman:	*(interrupting)* But you say it's a Magic Mender. Why do I need a Magic Mender just to put my skirt back together? You're just trying to get my egg money away from me.
Pedlar:	Come now, come now. Suspicious? That's not like you, not like the new you.
Old Woman:	*(softening)* It's true. I do need to be put together. But do I really need a Magic Mender to do it?
Pedlar:	You said it yourself – you need to be put together. It's not only your skirt that needs putting together, is it?
Old Woman:	*(thinks)* No, that's true…well, all right. I'll buy it! Here's your money.
	She pays him, and he gives her the Magic Mender. The Old Woman reads the instructions on the tag.
	Oh, dear!
Pedlar:	What's wrong?
Old Woman:	You said it pleats, smocks, stitches, darns and mends all in one silent operation. It says here you must be silent to make it work. It says: "Noiseless as hope, silence is the power. It's all in the way you hold your tongue." What does that mean? Just when all my hopes were raised. I'm beyond hope now.
Hope:	*(entering)* No one is ever beyond me. I'm still here.
Old Woman:	Oh, Hope, I didn't mean to take your name in vain. I'm really doing awfully well. I stood on my own feet, and I fought my own fight. I found my – no, my dog found me. I found my skirt.
	The Mute enters, sweeping.
	Now I just have to get my skirt back on, and I may find out exactly who I am, but…
Hope:	But what?
Old Woman:	I can't follow the directions for the Magic Mender.
Hope:	What do they say?

Old Woman:	*(reads again)* "Noiseless as hope, silence is the power. It's all in the way you hold your tongue."
Hope:	Silence, you say?
Pedlar:	Silence, you say?
Old Woman:	Oh! Silence!

> *The Mute is balancing his broom on his finger. They all three look at him ,and he stops, double-takes, looks around him and does a 'who, me?' gesture.*

Oh, dear boy! I'd be so grateful if you would help me get my skirt back on. Would you please help me?

> *The Mute nods happily.*

Oh, that's so nice of you.

> *She hands over the skirt and the Magic Mender to the Mute, who reads the label and holds up a finger to mean 'Stop!'*

What?

> *The Mute points to Hope, then to himself, then to the skirt and to the Old Woman.*

Old Woman:	You need Hope?

> *The Mute nods.*

Hope:	Everyone does. Everything that is done in the world is done with Hope.
Pedlar:	*(shouts)* Well, get on with it, then!
Old Woman & Hope:	

Shhhh!!!

> *The Mute pantomimes with them.*

> *In silence, the Mute and Hope fix the shirt – Velcro – attaching it and cranking the Magic Mender to fix it back on. The Pedlar maintains the silence and keeps the audience hushed, if necessary.*

Old Woman:	Oh, thank you, thank you, thank you. You did a lovely job!

> *She whirls around.*

Look at me, look at me! Oh, I do feel more like myself again…whoever I am. Oh, dear! I still don't know my name!

Pedlar:	Isn't anything coming back to you?

The Old Woman shakes her head miserably.

Don't lose hope.

Hope: I'm not lost. I'm right here.

The Mute comes to her and signals.

Old Woman: Another charade? My, you talk a lot.

The Mute starts: ten words – The message is "A rose by any other name would smell as sweet." Hope leaps in and guesses it quickly at the third or fourth word.

A rose by any other name would smell as sweet. But I don't know any other name for a rose...tea rose, cabbage rose, rose hip, rose water, rosedale...rosemary...Rosemary...that's it!

The Old Woman goes to each of them in turn, shakes hands.

How do you do, I'm Rosemary...how do you do, I'm Rosemary...how do you do, I'm Rosemary...Well, now that we all know each other, do you know what I'm going to do now?

Pedlar: Tell us.

Rosemary: I'm going to invite the three of you to come home with me for scrambled eggs – right now!

Pedlar: Good! Because now is where you are.

Rosemary: Or my name isn't Rosemary. And it is.

Pedlar: Is what?

Rosemary: Rosemary!

The End

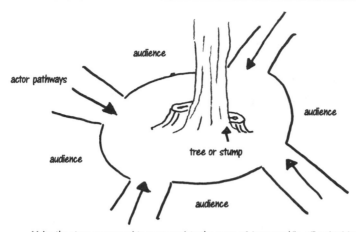

Make the stage area round to accommodate the sense of journey while still maintaining the illusion of not really getting anywhere

The tree could be a ladder with leaves or just some sturdy boxes covered or painted – areas which will offer the actors different levels to play on

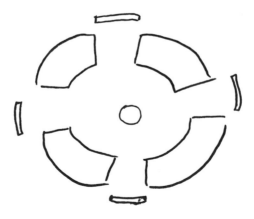

top view of set

Assuming that actors may play multiple parts, change areas can be provided for

acting space

audience

Perhaps some of the characters could be puppets which would mean the set could be like this

The journey could be simulated by moving a panorama across the puppet space

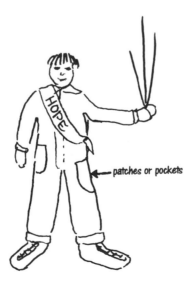

patches or pockets

Costume idea
Put all of the characters the Old Woman meets in workmen's overalls - the accessories (hats, bags, etc..) identify characters (maybe banners as well)
perhaps add colorful sneakers as well

The Old Woman

Quenten Doolittle

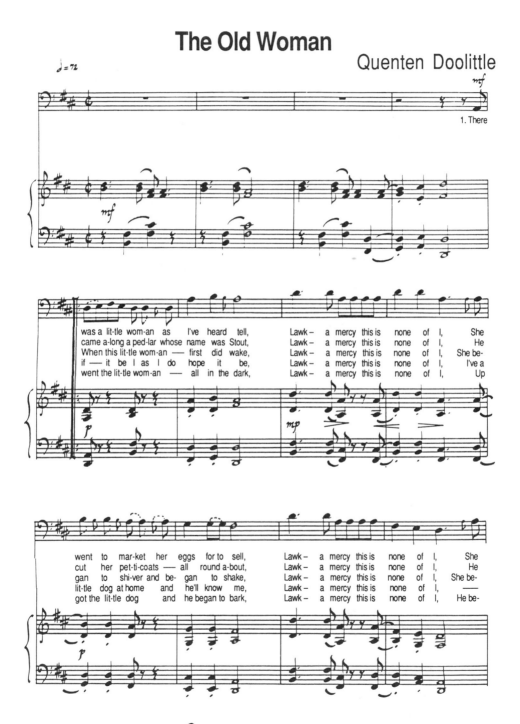

was a lit-tle wom-an as I've heard tell, Lawk – a mercy this is none of I, She
came a-long a ped-lar whose name was Stout, Lawk – a mercy this is none of I, He
When this lit-tle wom-an — first did wake, Lawk – a mercy this is none of I, She be-
if — it be I as I do hope it be, Lawk – a mercy this is none of I, I've a
went the lit-tle wom-an — all in the dark, Lawk – a mercy this is none of I, Up

went to mar-ket her eggs for to sell, Lawk – a mercy this is none of I, She
cut her pet-ti-coats — all round a-bout, Lawk – a mercy this is none of I, He
gan to shi-ver and be- gan to shake, Lawk – a mercy this is none of I, She be-
lit-tle dog at home and he'll know me, Lawk – a mercy this is none of I, —
got the lit-tle dog and he began to bark, Lawk – a mercy this is none of I, He be-

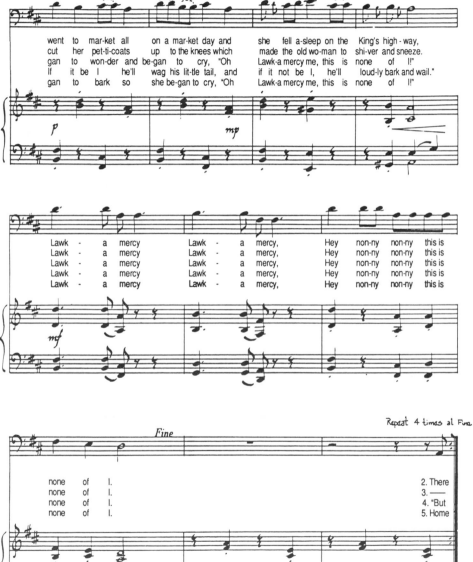

went to mar-ket all | on a mar-ket day and | she fell a-sleep on the | King's high-way,
cut her pet-ti-coats | up to the knees which | made the old wo-man to | shi-ver and sneeze.
gan to won-der and | be-gan to cry, "Oh | Lawk-a mercy me, this is | none of I!"
If it be I | he'll wag his lit-tle tail, and | if it not be I, | he'll loud-ly bark and wail."
gan to bark so | she be-gan to cry, "Oh | Lawk-a mercy me, this is | none of I!"

Lawk - a mercy | Lawk - a mercy, | Hey non-ny non-ny this is
Lawk - a mercy | Lawk - a mercy, | Hey non-ny non-ny this is
Lawk - a mercy | Lawk - a mercy, | Hey non-ny non-ny this is
Lawk - a mercy | Lawk - a mercy, | Hey non-ny non-ny this is
Lawk - a mercy | Lawk - a mercy, | Hey non-ny non-ny this is

Fine

Repeat 4 times al Fine

none of I. | 2. There
none of I. | 3. ——
none of I. | 4. "But
none of I. | 5. Home

The Merchants of Dazu

JAMES DEFELICE

Design Concept by Douglas McCullough

JAMES DEFELICE has written for stage, film, television and radio. His screenplay for *Why Shoot the Teacher* received an Etrog Award at the 1977 Canadian Film Awards, and he has recently coauthored, with Alberta filmmaker Anne Wheeler, the screenplay for *Angel Square*. His *Letting Go*, broadcast on the CBC series "The Way We Are," was honoured at the San Francisco Film Festival. He received an Alberta Achievement Award in Theatre Arts in 1978. James DeFelice is a member of the Department of Drama at the University of Alberta, where he teaches acting and directing and where he directs numerous professional and university productions.

The Merchants of Dazu was first performed by Chinook Theatre, Edmonton, Alberta, from February 15 - May 15, 1984, and at the Edmonton International Children's Festival, May 17 - 18, 1984, with the following cast:

Narrator 1   Joanne Wilson
Narrator 2   Marianne Copithorne (February 15 - April 6)
Narrator 2   Anne McGrath (April 7 - May 19)
Hua   Kent Staines
Aw Boo   Jean-Raymond Chales
Stage Manager/Percussion   P. Susanah Windrum

Directed by Brian Paisley
Designed by Daniel Van Heyst
Music by Jamie Philp
Masks by Heather Redfern

CHARACTERS
Narrator 1
Narrator 2
Hua
Aw Boo
Stage Manager/Percussion

PLACE
China

TIME
The distant past.

The Merchants of Dazu

Open stage. Wooden pillars up Right and Left are connected by a canvas screen. The title of the play, "The Merchants of Dazu," is painted on it over a simple map of ancient China showing the important places cited in the play. As the Merchants travel from place to place, the Narrators rotate the canvas screen to indicate the specific local. The canvas should be painted in the style of ancient Chinese art.

As the audience enters, the Stage Manager, dressed in black, is Down Left, playing a row of "found" percussion instruments which includes bottles, pottery and glass jars, and pipes.

The two Narrators, dressed simply in Chinese garments evocative of the past, sit on raised area Up Right and Up Left. If a suitable stringed instrument (ie. a Cheng) can be found, one of the Narrators plucks the instrument.

Narrator 2 indicates the start of the play by striking a small gong.

Narrator 1 rises and addresses the audience. Narrator 2 can continue plucking the stringed instrument or playing the flute behind the Narrator 1's speech.

Music from the Stage Manager and the Narrators can underscore the action and songs throughout the play.

Narrator 1: We are back many hundreds of years in ancient China. Two merchants have set out from Dazu, also known as Shanghai, a large city on the South China Sea. The merchants want to travel north across the Yangtze River to the Great Wall and all the way to the Gobi Desert.

    Indicates on map.

What do the merchants plan to do on their long journey? You will see.

    Suddenly a loud crashing sound is heard. Enter the two Merchants pushing and pulling a wooden wagon onto the stage. Hua, the tall thin merchant, is pulling the wagon. Aw Boo, the short rotund merchant, is pushing the wagon. Both wear ragged cloaks. The wagon is empty. Aw Boo gives the wagon one last shove, knocking Hua to the ground.

Hua: *(in pain)* Ahhh. Watch what you are doing!

Aw Boo: Your fault.

Hua:	*(trying to get up, he falls back down again)* Look where you are going.
Aw Boo:	I *was* looking. You're too slow.
Hua:	*(starts to curl up on the ground)* I'm tired.
Aw Boo:	*(goes to him)* Up! Up! Up!

> *Aw Boo pulls Hua to his feet. But Hua's momentum pushes them both to the ground in an almost double somersault.*

You clumsy fool!

> *Jumps back up.*

Hua:	*(from a supine position)* Why don't we have a horse?
Aw Boo:	*(angry)* Why don't we have a horse!
Hua:	That's what I just asked you.
Aw Boo:	I'm not deaf.
Hua:	If we had a horse, we wouldn't have to pull this wagon.
Aw Boo:	*(angrier)* If we had a horse, we would look too rich. No one would sell us anything.

> *Pulls Hua from the ground.*

Come on, Hua, we must reach Hangzhou by sunset. There we will find Longjing tea. The best in all China.

Hua:	But I can't move another step.
Aw Boo:	Then I will pull you.

> *Picks up Hua and pushes him into the wagon.*

And you will pull me tomorrow.

> *Aw Boo starts to pull the wagon. His movement is stylized and he walks in place as if pulling Hua in the wagon.*

> *Narrator 1 pulls screen to reveal a painted scene of outside a large city.*

> *Hua beats a small drum.*

Hua & Aw Boo: *(singing)* We are from the city, we are wise.
We will travel to the small towns and villages.
We will buy the treasures from the people we meet.
We will pay them very little.
Because they do not know their true value.
But we are from the city and we are wise.

	We will fill our wagon with tea and silk and jade and ivory.
Hua:	*(greedily)* Yes!
Aw Boo:	We will sell these treasures in our city of Dazu. We will become wealthy men.
Hua:	Yes! Yes!
	Stops beating his drum.
	And then can we buy a horse?
Aw Boo:	When the wagon is full.
	Light change. Aw Boo and Hua are sleeping beside the wagon. Narrator 2 pulls screen to reveal a mountainous region with mist in the distance. Narrator 1 puts on the mask and dress of the Lady Who Picks Tea. She works in an almost dance-like motion.
	Aw Boo wakes. He sees the Lady. He watches the woman work for a moment. Aw Boo shakes Hua to wake him.
Hua:	*(sits up, opens his eyes, shuts them and falls back asleep with a snore)* Wake me up at noon.
Aw Boo:	*(shakes him)* We will never become rich sleeping until noon. See! There is our first catch.
Hua:	*(sees the Lady)* A woman. Only takes one fisherman.
	Flops back to sleep.
Aw Boo:	*(angry, shakes Hua harder)* Wake up! Or I'll make you pull the wagon all the way to the Great Wall.
	Pushes Hua.
	Remember our plan!
Hua:	*(pulls himself together and walks over to the Lady)* Excuse me, my good woman.
Lady:	*(straightens up)* I can't talk to you. I must finish picking the tea leaves before the sun is too hot.
Hua:	*(sneering)* The leaves look too small.
Lady:	*(hurt)* They are very tender leaves.
Hua:	Colour is not good.
Lady:	These leaves make the best tea in the region.
Hua:	Then the region produces bad tea.

Lady:	*(losing confidence)* Smell the leaf.
Hua:	*(smells and feigns sickness)* Putrid. The stink of dead fish.
Lady:	Taste the leaf.
Hua:	*(tastes and feigns spitting out the leaf)* Bitter. Tastes like rotting weeds.
Lady:	*(confused)* But no one's ever complained about our tea before.
Hua:	*(with conceit)* Has anyone from Dazu ever tasted your tea?
Lady:	Dazu?
Hua:	Yes. I have the experience of a man from the city.

> *Looks at her.*

> But you have the face of an honest worker. I will help you sell your inferior tea.

Lady:	*(smiles weakly)* Thank you.
Hua:	*(feigns speaking confidentially)* My friend…

> *Pointing to Aw Boo.*

> actually, I don't really like him…has no taste for tea. I will tell him the tea is better than it is.

Lady:	*(smiles weakly)* Yes.
Hua:	Bring those bags over here.

> *Lady starts to pull bags. Hua gives Aw Boo a signal when her back is turned.*

Aw Boo:	*(walking over to Lady)* Have you any tea for sale?
Hua:	*(interrupts before Lady can speak)* Yes, she has. Her tea is to your taste.
Aw Boo:	I can only pay one hundred Yuan.

> *Aw Boo starts to take money from bag. Lady raises her hand in protest. Hua interrupts her again.*

Hua:	That is a very fair price.

> *Lady is reluctant. Hua whispers to her.*

> You will never get a higher price. His taste buds are not as refined as mine.

Lady:	Yes.
Aw Boo:	*(counts out his money)* We might buy more of your tea. If we pass

through here again.

Loads bags of tea onto the wagon.

Hua: How do we reach the river from here?

Lady: *(pointing)* Through that pass in the mountains.

Hua picks up the front of the wagon.

But be very careful not to take the high road. The mist forms without warning. And it could be very dangerous.

Lady exits holding money.

Narrator 1 takes off mask and puts it by her side. She takes her position on the raised level up stage.

Hua is now pulling the wagon. Aw Boo is standing on the wagon with the bags of tea. Hua walks in place with the wagon.

Aw Boo: One hundred Yuan for this tea. We will sell it for fifty times more in the city. Longjing is the Emperor's favourite tea.

Hua: *(as he walks in place)* Imagine her not knowing the value of her tea.

Aw Boo: I tell you we will become rich on this journey.

Aw Boo starts to beat the drum. Narrator 1 pulls screen to reveal Yangtze River.

While Narrator 1 speaks, Narrator 2 puts on the mask of the Ferryman. Narrator 2 ties sash under trousers and around waist and pulls up trousers to knee length.

Narrator 1: The merchants, pleased with their first conquest, make their way safely through the mountain pass. The advice of the Lady Who Picks Tea saves them from the dangerous mist. The Merchants arrive at the shore of the Yangtze River. There they meet the Ferryman who takes people across the swirling and silt-laden river on his large junk.

Ferryman rolls out a large bamboo mat which will represent the ferry. He takes a long bamboo pole which has been leaning against the back of the stage.

The Merchants enter pulling their wagon. Aw Boo stops pulling the wagon. He sees the pieces of jade (represented by green-painted rocks) on the ferry and is amazed.

Hua: *(standing in the wagon, amazed at the sight of the jade)* Do you see that jade?

Aw Boo:	I am not without eyes. I have never seen jade so exquisite. So translucent.
Hua:	The sun shines through it like a blaze.
	Overly eager.
	We must buy some.
Aw Boo:	*(holding Hua back)* Wait! Not so eager! The largest fish goes to the patient angler.
Hua:	*(almost to himself)* How did a poor ferryman find such jade?
	The audience imagines the beauty of the jade through the eyes of the characters.
Aw Boo:	Look, there – a rich emerald green. And there – a milky white. This is imperial jade and fit only for an emperor.
Ferryman:	*(sees them)* Good day, travelers.
Hua:	*(feigning coldness)* What is so good about today?
Ferryman:	*(cheerful)* The sun rose this morning. The birds are singing. And the monsoon rains have not yet come.
Aw Boo:	We are not here for conversation. Only to be ferried across this river.
Ferryman:	I'll take you for four Yuan.
Hua:	*(starts to agree, takes coins from his purse)* Yes, that would be a fair –
Aw Boo:	*(interrupting, pulls Hua's arm back)* Four Yuan. Who do you think we are?
Ferryman:	*(looks at them)* Merchants.
Aw Boo:	Not rich merchants who live in the large cities. We are poor. We eke out our meager living by walking the back roads of vast country.
Hua:	And besides we have no horse.
Ferryman:	I noticed.
	Thinks for a moment.
	Well, since you have no horse…three Yuan.
Aw Boo:	Agreed!
Ferryman:	Pull your wagon on my ferry!
	Aw Boo and Hua pull the wagon on the bamboo mat.

Ferryman: Watch out!

        Rocks back and forth, indicating the movement of the ferry on the river, balancing himself with his long bamboo pole.

You are pulling the wagon too near the side. And the water is very deep now.

        Aw Boo and Hua move the wagon into place. They walk unsteadily on the bamboo mat as if they were on a ferry on a quickly moving river. The Ferryman begins to mime the movement of the ferry across the Yangtze. He sings as he guides the boat.

Ferryman: *(sings)* My precious jewel of a river,
In all China the most wide.
Protect us from the killing floods –
Take us safely to your other side.

        Hua and Aw Boo weave back and forth as the boat makes its trip.

Have you ever ridden on this river before?

Aw Boo: No, we are from another place.

Ferryman: Why do you come here?

Aw Boo: To buy. To sell.

        Slyly.

Do you have anything to sell?

Ferryman: Only my back. And my arms. To guide you across this river.

Hua: What about that jade?

Ferryman: *(speaks while guiding the ferry with his pole)* You are interested in my jade?

Aw Boo: *(playing indifferent)* Maybe. Maybe we'll look at it.

        Ferryman hands Aw Boo the jade. Aw Boo can hardly contain himself as he handles it.

Ferryman: A camel train carried this jade from the Sinkiang Province. They were carrying the jade to Xian. To the Emperor's burial grounds.

Aw Boo: They were?

Ferryman: The camel drivers wanted to cross the river. I told them it was too dangerous. The floods had carried tons of silt down the river. The bottom of the river was high with silt.

Aw Boo: Yes?

Ferryman: The camel drivers tried to cross the river at a shallow place. But they were swept away by the rushing waters.

Hua: They drowned?

Ferryman: No. I saved them and their camels and their cargo. As a reward they gave me the jade.

Aw Boo: This jade?

Ferryman: The piece you are holding is called the Jewel of Heaven.

Aw Boo: Very inferior.

Hua: *(picking up his cue)* Yes, worthless.

Ferryman: No!

Aw Boo: *(laughs mockingly)* My friend, the camel drivers played a joke on you.

Hua: This is more coloured rock than jade. You might as well throw it all back in the river.

             Feigns that he is going to throw a piece in the river.

Ferryman: *(stopping him)* No!

             Looks at the jade.

             But it is so beautiful.

Aw Boo: Not to us.

Hua: The camel drivers have convinced you this trash is beautiful. So you think it is.

Aw Boo: They have put a spell on you.

             The Ferryman reaches shore. Hua and Aw Boo jostle back as the ferry touches the shore. Hua and Aw Boo push the wagon onto the shore.

Aw Boo: If anyone else saw your "jade," they would laugh at you.

Hua: Yes, laugh till they were sore.

Ferryman: *(confused)* You are merchants. You should know.

Hua: Yes.

Aw Boo: But we would never buy your…

             Laughs.

         jade.

Ferryman:	*(scratches his head)* And they told me it was valuable.
Aw Boo:	But we are not heartless men.
Hua:	Yes.
Aw Boo:	Because you have taken us safely across the river, we might help you.
Ferryman:	How?
Aw Boo:	By trading something for your worthless rock.
Hua:	Because we are merchants, we will be able to trade your fool's jade for something else on our travels.
Aw Boo:	And we will help save you from further ridicule.
Ferryman:	*(disgusted with himself)* I should throw all this in the river.
	Aw Boo and Hua are alarmed. They nearly lose their composure as they rush to stop the Ferryman from throwing the jade in the river.
Aw Boo:	That will not be necessary!
Hua:	We will trade you something useful for it.
Aw Boo:	*(surprised)* What?
Hua:	Tea!
	Looks at the wagon.
Aw Boo:	Yes.
	Takes a burlap bag of tea from wagon.
	Longjing tea. Fit for an emperor.
Ferryman:	I have heard of this famous tea but never tasted it.
Aw Boo:	The tea is yours…in exchange for the "jade."
	Hua starts to put the pieces of jade into the empty burlap bags. He can hardly contain his joy.
Ferryman:	I feel sorry that I am giving you such a poor exchange.
Hua:	We are always happy to help our fellow man.
	The Ferryman begins to push his boat away from the shore.
Aw Boo:	Enjoy your tea!
	Narrator 2 takes off the mask of the Ferryman. Narrator 1 rolls up bamboo mat that served as the ferry and places pole and mat in upstage position.

Hua:	I am sorry we had to give up a bag of tea.
Au Boo:	*(laughs loudly)* All the bags of tea we have ever seen are not worth this jade. We are wealthy men. And sooner than I would have dreamed. The carvings made from this jade *will* be fit for an emperor's tomb – or better, an emperor's palace.
Hua:	Maybe we should go back?
Aw Boo:	*(stops)* What?
Hua:	Go back to our city. We are rich now. We do not need anything more.
Aw Boo:	*(starts moving in place at a faster pace)* We have just started. Before we are done, this wagon will be filled to overflowing.

Aw Boo and Hua pull the wagon behind the screens. Hua has a troubled look on his face as he exits.

Stage Manager and Narrator 1 play musical transition. Narrator 2 moves the canvas screen revealing a picture of the bamboo forests. He then moves towards the audience.

Narrator 2:	Hua and Aw Boo continue their journey. They fill their wagon with the treasures of each region traded to them for almost nothing in return. They have reached the bamboo forests of the north.

Wagon enters pulled by both Aw Boo and Hua.

Hua:	*(straining under the load)* When will we buy a horse?
Aw Boo:	*(also straining)* When the wagon is filled.
Hua:	We have enough already.
Aw Boo:	I want more.

Merchants collapse on the ground, breathing heavily.

	There is a way we can more quickly fill the wagon.
Hua:	*(lying on the ground, exhausted)* How?
Aw Boo:	*(takes out his map)* See, the road divides in two.
Hua:	Yes?
Aw Boo:	We will also divide. That way to gain twice the treasures. You will follow this road to find silk. I will follow that road to find porcelain.
Hua:	Good idea!

Starts to walk down the road, then turns suddenly.

| | What about the wagon? |
| Aw Boo: | I will take care of the wagon. |

Hua stands staring at Aw Boo as he begins to pull the wagon down the other road.

Stops.

What's the matter? Do you not trust me?

| Hua: | *(voice has imploring tone)* You will not leave me out here alone? |
| Aw Boo: | We will meet on the other side of the Great Wall. |

Hua starts to walk down the road. Aw Boo calls after him.

Remember. Silk.

He throws a burlap bag which Hua catches.

Use this for trading.

Aw Boo exits down Right Stage road pulling the wagon.

During the last sequence the Narrators 1 and 2 have put on the masks of the Silk Ladies. They sing a melody without words and mime the winding off and weaving of silk thread. Beside them are two bundles that represent silk.

Hua:	*(watches them a moment before speaking)* Hello!
Silk Lady 1:	Don't talk to us now!
Silk Lady 2:	We have to pull the thread off the cocoon.
Hua:	Cocoon?
Silk Lady 1:	Of the silk worm.
Silk Lady 2:	There is a mile of thread here that must be wound off and woven.
Hua:	*(laughs)* Who would want the thread of a worm?
Silk Lady 1:	It is very valuable.
Silk Lady 2:	We feed the worm mulberry leaves, and the worm rewards us with silk.
Hua:	Who told you that?
Silk Lady 1:	The men who buy the silk from us. They take the silk in caravans many thousands of miles from here.
Hua:	You have woven many miles of silk.
Silk Lady 2:	The silk is the finest in China. In ancient times, the wives of

the Roman Emperors wore dresses made from our silk.

Silk Lady 1: *(speaks as she works)* And our rulers use the silk as gifts to the people in the west who want to conquer us.

Hua: *(laughs)* Your rulers weaken the enemy by giving them a taste of luxury.

Silk Lady 2: *(as she works)* Why are you so interested in our silk?

Hua: I am a merchant.

Silk Lady 1: We only trade with the caravans.

Hua: I have something that the caravans want...

> *Holds up the burlap bag.*

even more than silk.

Silk Lady 1: *(stops working)* More than silk?

Hua: The finest jade in the world.

Silk Lady 2: *(stops working)* Jade?

Hua: *(opens bag)* Look!

Silk Lady 1: *(takes jade out of bag and holds it up to the sun)* I am dazzled by the colour.

Silk Lady 2: I have never seen such jade. Is there a fire burning inside?

Hua: One piece is worth more than all your silk. But if you do not want the jade, I will give you money or tea. Longjing tea.

Silk Lady 1: My reason tells me no. But your jade dazzles my senses.

Silk Lady 2: And mine too.

Hua: This piece of jade will make you rich. I will trade it for your silk because I am traveling to a place where silk is more valuable than jade.

Silk Lady 2: If you had told me you were going to a place where jade is more valuable than silk, I would not have believed you.

Silk Lady 1: He is an honest man.

> *Both women seem to be hypnotized by the gleaming green jade which Hua holds in front of them.*

Silk Lady 2: We will trade our silk for your jade.

> *Hua gives the Silk Ladies the jade. He picks up two or three bundles of the silk in his arms.*

Hua: *(struggles with the silk, almost to himself he speaks)* I wish I had that wagon now.

            Starts to walk away. He turns.

            How do I find my way to the Great Wall?

Silk Lady 2:   We will show you. But you must be very careful in the bamboo forests.

Silk Lady 1:   There are ferocious animals that the gods have put there to protect the sacred pandas.

            The Women lead Hua off as he struggles under the weight of his silk.

Hua: *(stops for a moment, speaks to himself)* Will Aw Boo and the wagon be at the Great Wall? Or has Aw Boo left with the wagon and its treasures for himself?

            The Narrators take off the masks of the Silk Ladies. Narrator 1 moves the screen to reveal the drawing of the Great Wall. Narrator 2 underscores the opening of the scene with flute music before exiting behind the screen to prepare for the playing of the Watchtower Guard.

Narrator 1:   Aw Boo had thought about taking the treasures in the wagon for himself. But he changed his mind when he realized how difficult it was for one person to pull the wagon. And besides, there was still some space left in the wagon for more treasures.

            Aw Boo enters pulling the wagon. It is more laden than when last seen.

Narrator 1:   Aw Boo waits by the Great Wall for Hua.

            Hua enters with burden of silk. Aw Boo sees him. He is pleased. Aw Boo rushes to help Hua.

Aw Boo: Congratulations, Hua. You have succeeded!

            Looks at silk. He is impressed.

            The silk is the most beautiful I have ever seen.

Hua: The mulberry leaves are the best in China. The silk worm feeds well.

            Aw Boo loads the silk onto the wagon.

Aw Boo: Good!

            Speaks with enthusiasm as he loads the silk on the wagon.

            The sun was shining on my fortune, too.

Points into the wagon.

Porcelain vases, gold jeweled plaques, fan paintings, lacquer gift boxes. And all for a fraction of their worth. The people here do not know the value of what they trade. But we are from Dazu. We know the worth of things.

Hua: Now we can return to Dazu.

Aw Boo: But we are not finished!

Hua: If we put more treasures in the wagon, we will not be able to pull it.

Aw Boo: *(dismissing him)* We will buy only light treasures.

            A figure appears at a high level which represents one of the watchtowers of the Great Wall. The Watchtower Guard, played by the Narrator 2, could be on a ladder or platform behind the screen with the drawing of the Great Wall.

Guard: Who stands before the Great Wall?

Aw Boo: *(turns toward the Guard)* Two peaceful men.

Guard: Do you wish to pass through the gates?

Aw Boo: Yes!

Guard: Who are you?

Aw Boo: Poor merchants.

Guard: Where are you going?

Aw Boo: North. To the Gobi desert.

Hua: *(surprised to hear this)* The Gobi desert? Why are we –?

Aw Boo: *(under his breath)* Silence!

Guard: What is in your wagon?

Aw Boo: *(lifts rough burlap cover a few inches and peeks underneath it)* A few worthless goods we have gathered on our travels.

Guard: I will open the gate for you –

Aw Boo: How much will that cost?

Guard: Nothing to travel north –

Aw Boo: *(to Hua, very pleased)* Nothing. Think of it.

Guard: But –

Hua: But, what?

Aw Boo:	*(to Hua)* Do not ask that. He might change his mind.
Hua:	*(quickly)* You're right.
Aw Boo:	*(to Guard)* We are ready to pass through the gates.
	In stylized movement, the large wooden gates of the Great Wall are opened. This action can be performed symbolically with a movement of the screen showing the image of the other side of the Wall and Aw Boo and Hua pivoting the wagon.
	Aw Boo and Hua pull the wagon with difficulty. Aw Boo pants from the effort.
Aw Boo:	You are right, Hua, the time has come to buy a horse.
Guard:	*(joining them on the other side of the Wall)* Do you plan to pull your wagon all the way to the desert?
Aw Boo:	We would like to buy a horse. I see you have several of them grazing by the wall.
Guard:	Those are very good horses. Mongolians. Very strong. Able to travel twenty-five miles a day in the coldest weather without tiring.
Aw Boo:	*(pointing)* I like that one. With the long mane. And the ribbons.
Guard:	You have very good taste in horses. He is yours for –
Aw Boo:	We could trade you some tea.
Guard:	No.
Aw Boo:	Beautiful silk?
	Guard shakes his head.
	A piece of exquisite jade?
Guard:	No.
Aw Boo:	What then?
Guard:	Two sacks of rice!
Aw Boo:	*(surprised)* Rice?
Guard:	Two sacks and the horse is yours –
Aw Boo:	*(quietly pleased with himself)* Yes –
	To Hua.
	Quick, Hua, the rice.

Hua goes to the wagon and takes out two sacks of rice. The Guard eagerly takes the sacks.

Guard: And here is your horse.

The Guard leads the Mongolian horse, represented by a wooden horse's head or mask on a pole held by the Narrator 1 who mimes all the movements of the horse. The horse has ribbons coming off the mane and is ornately decorated. The horse is spirited, but Aw Boo and the Guard manage to tie it to the wagon.

Aw Boo: *(to himself)* A magnificent animal –

Guard: Good luck on your journey.

Guard exits with two sacks of rice. Narrator 1 holds horse head with one hand and pulls the wagon with the other. Hua pushes the wagon from behind.

Aw Boo: *(very pleased with himself)* Two sacks of rice! And he could have had tea, silk, jade. The two sacks of rice are the most worthless items in our wagon.

Hua: *(weakly)* Why are we going to the desert?

Aw Boo: To buy the finest stoneware tea bowls in all China.

Hua: *(incredulous)* Tea bowls?

Aw Boo: Made in the kilns on the edge of the desert. Only here the craftsmen know the secret process of making tea bowls with the thick black glaze which gives such a rare taste to the tea brewed in them. To the Japanese tea masters, these bowls are more precious than gold.

Hua: Yes?

Aw Boo: And they will give us gold for them.

Horse pulls the wagon, walking in place. Aw Boo and Hua walk in place beside the wagon as music from the Stage Manager underscores their long journey to the north.

Narrator 2 has taken off the mask of the Guard and speaks to the audience.

Narrator 2:   Aw Boo drives the horse faster and faster, so impatient is he to reach the kilns that touch the desert.

In a stylized mime, Aw Boo, Hua and the Horse echo the description of the Narrator.

When Aw Boo sees the smoke and fire coming from the kilns, he can hardly contain his joy. He does not yet feel the bitter winds which blow across the desert from coldest Siberia.

The music continues to underscore the following actions:

Narrator 2 puts on the mask of the Maker of Tea Bowls.

Without dialogue, Aw Boo's bartering for the tea bowls is acted out. He finally convinces the Maker to take some silk and some tea for the bowls.

After the transaction, Narrator 2 takes off the mask of the Maker of Tea Bowls.

The Horse continues to walk in place pulling the wagon.

Narrator 2:   The merchants have filled the wagon with treasures. Now they can enjoy the fruits of their work.

Aw Boo: *(stopping the Horse and speaking with pure ecstasy of satisfaction)* We have done it, Hua!

Hua: Yes.

Aw Boo: And you wanted to turn back.

Hua: *(pats the Horse's mane., the Horse responds with satisfaction)* I'm glad we have the horse.

   Aw Boo starts to take off his cloak.

   What are you doing? It is too cold.

Aw Boo: *(climbs on the wagon)* I have been showing the world only my rags. Now the world should see my wealth.

   Aw Boo turns his cloak of rags inside out. The other side reveals a cloak of furs and jewels. He wears the cloak proudly and stands tall in the wagon.

   Hua looks at his cloak which is rags on both sides. He sits in the back of the wagon.

   Aw Boo begins to sing. Hua beats the drum and joins him in his singing chant.

Hua & Aw Boo: We were ordinary merchants of Dazu.
   We lived from day to day.
   Never knowing when our pockets would be full.
   Never knowing when our pockets would be empty.
   Then we took a long journey.
   Our wagon was empty.
   But our heads were full of wisdom.
   And now our wagon is filled to overflowing.
   Come horse, take us swiftly back to Dazu.

We will return to our city.
The richest merchants in China.

> *Lights fade on Aw Boo and his triumphant pose on top of the wagon, wearing his fur and jeweled cloak.*
>
> *Sound of wind, a cold wind; it can be made by one of the Narrators blowing on a wind instrument.*
>
> *Lights up on Aw Boo and Hua huddled next to the wagon. They have pulled their cloaks around them for warmth. The Horse is shivering from the cold, too.*

Hua: (*as he shivers*) We need a fire.

Aw Boo: Who would have thought the desert nights would be so cold.

Hua: There are no trees for firewood.

Aw Boo: (*stands, looks about him*) Only sand. Everywhere sand.

Hua: What happened to our wood?

Aw Boo: Wood?

Hua: That we kept in the wagon.

Aw Boo: (*doesn't want to answer*) I don't know.

Hua: We had six logs.

Aw Boo: (*suddenly*) I traded the wood for porcelain.

Hua: But –

Aw Boo: Porcelain is precious. Wood is almost worthless.

Hua: Except when there are no trees.

Aw Boo: Huddle close to the horse for warmth.

> *They move close to the horse.*

The horse is cold, too.

Hua: We could burn the wagon.

Aw Boo: Then how could we carry our treasures to Dazu?

Hua: Better than freezing here.

> *Narrator 2 enters and puts on the mask of the Maker of Tea Bowls.*

Maker: Merchants, you will never last this night.

Aw Boo: Do you have wood?

Maker:	No.
Aw Boo:	How do you keep warm?
Maker:	From the fires burning in my kilns.
Hua:	Yes, we will warm ourselves next to your kilns.
	Starts to lead the horse to the kilns.
Maker:	Not so fast!
	Aw Boo and Hua stop.
	You are merchants. You understand trade.
Aw Boo:	*(impatient)* Yes?
Maker:	The heat of my kilns is not something I give away.
Aw Boo:	What do you mean?
Maker:	I will trade you the heat of my kilns for something in your wagon.
Aw Boo:	*(irritated)* What?
Maker:	Your silk. All of it.
Aw Boo:	*(angry)* Our silk!
Maker:	And all of your tea.
Aw Boo:	We would be trading something for nothing. Keep your heat.
Maker:	You will die out here. Only strangers to this region would ever travel at night without firewood.
Aw Boo:	I will not give up my silk and tea.
Hua:	He is right. We will not last the night.
Maker:	At least one of you has common sense.
	Aw Boo looks at the silk and tea. He is making up his mind.
Hua:	We will die.
Aw Boo:	*(pulls his cloak around him)* We have no choice. Take what you want. And lead us to your warming ovens.
	The Maker takes the silk and the remaining bags of tea from the wagon.
	A special light of reds and yellows gives the area a feeling of flame and warmth.
	Aw Boo, Hua and the Horse hover around the light for warmth.

Stage Manager plays music under the following scene. Narrator 2 takes off the mask of the Maker of Tea Bowls.

Hua leads wagon and Horse around the stage and behind the canvas screen. Aw Boo walks behind, despondent over the loss of some of his treasures.

Narrator 2:   No silk or tea remain in the wagon. But Aw Boo and Hua have survived the bitter cold desert night.

Gestures to the mask of the Maker of Tea Bowls.

Thanks to the Maker of Tea Bowls.

Pulls the screen to reveal the Great Wall.

But during the journey from the Gobi Desert, Aw Boo and Hua have used up their food. They are very hungry.

Hua: *(collapsing)* I cannot go another step without food.

Aw Boo: There should have been wild ducks and geese for food. But we haven't seen one.

Hua: Are we lost?

Aw Boo: I don't know where we are.

Hua: Is that the same as being lost?

Aw Boo: *(suddenly, at a distance, sees something and is happy)* Look! Over there!

Hua: *(looking at a distance in the direction Aw Boo is pointing)* The Great Wall!

Aw Boo: We will find food there.

Hua: And gain back our strength for the journey back to Dazu.

Narrator 2 puts on mask of the Watchtower Guard.

Guard: *(standing on higher level behind the canvas)* Who stands before the Great Wall?

Aw Boo: Two peaceful men.

Hua: Do you not remember us?

Guard: No. Do you wish to pass through the gates?

Aw Boo: Yes.

Guard: Where are you going?

Hua: South. To Dazu.

The Guard stares at them.

Aw Boo:	Aren't you going to open the gates?
Guard:	When you pay the toll.
Aw Boo:	But it cost nothing to travel north.
Guard:	To travel south will cost you fifty Yuan.
Aw Boo:	*(almost a tantrum)* Fifty Yuan. I will not pay it.
Guard:	Then stay where you are.
Hua:	We must pay the toll. We will starve here. I will pay it from my pocket.

Holds up the fifty Yuan.

Open the gate.

The Guard pulls the screen revealing the other side of the wall. Hua and Aw Boo pivot the horse and wagon. The Guard joins them on the other side of the wall. Hua hands him the money.

We are hungry.

Guard:	Have you no food?
Aw Boo:	*(still angry about the fifty Yuan)* If we had food, we would not be hungry.

Looks at the sky.

We thought we would be able to kill wild ducks and geese for our food.

Guard:	The wild fowl have all migrated south. To Dazu. Everyone knows that.
Hua:	*(weakly)* We didn't.
Aw Boo:	Do you have food?
Guard:	Yes. Rice.
Hua:	Can we have some?
Guard:	For trade.
Aw Boo:	*(pulls back cloth on wagon)* What do you want from us?
Guard:	Your horse.
Aw Boo:	But we need our horse.
Guard:	Then starve.

> *Starts to walk away.*

Aw Boo:	*(follows him)* We have jade. More precious than your rice.
Guard:	But you can't eat jade. Your horse or nothing.
Hua:	How much rice for our horse?
Guard:	Two cups.
Aw Boo:	But we traded two sacks for the horse.
Guard:	You were not hungry then. Two cups or nothing.
Hua:	We will take the two cups of rice.
Aw Boo:	*(close to a tantrum.)* No!
Hua:	We have no choice.

> *Hua detaches the Horse from the wagon. The Guard gives Hua and Aw Boo each a cup of rice. The Guard starts to lead away the Horse.*
>
> *Hua and Aw Boo devour their rice quickly. Their bowls are empty as they try to lick every grain from the bottom.*
>
> *The Guard turns to Hua and Aw Boo before exiting.*

Guard:	You could have eaten your horse.

> *Narrator 2 takes off the mask of the Watchtower Guard. Stage Manager plays music under the following scene.*
>
> *Narrator 2 pulls back the next screen revealing the bamboo forests and then changes into the mask and dress of the Silk Lady 2.*
>
> *Aw Boo and Hua push and pull the wagon.*

Hua:	We are in the region of the bamboo forests.

> *Narrator 1 joins the Narrator 2, having put on the mask of the Silk Lady 1.*

Hua:	Look, there are the women weaving the silk thread.

> *Silk Ladies sing as they work.*

Aw Boo:	Good, we can trade with them again. For the silk we lost. You said they gave you all that silk for one piece of jade.
Hua:	Yes.
Aw Boo:	Then two pieces of jade will bring twice as much.

> *The Silk Ladies continue to mime the winding off and weaving*

of silk thread. Hua approaches them.

Hua:	Hello!
Silk Lady 1:	Don't talk to us now!
Silk Lady 2:	We have to pull the thread off the cocoon.
Hua:	Don't you remember me?
Silk Lady 2:	No!
Aw Boo:	He traded jade with you. For silk.
Silk Lady 1:	We are too busy to remember.
Silk Lady 2:	We must finish the silk for the caravans that will be passing here soon.
Aw Boo:	You will not trade with us?
Silk Lady 1:	Not today.
Aw Boo:	There will not be another day. We travel south to Dazu.
Silk Lady 2:	Then watch out for the Sadnap monster.
Aw Boo:	*(stops in his tracks)* The Sadnap?
Silk Lady 1:	A ferocious beast that the gods have put in the bamboo forests to protect the pandas.
Aw Boo:	I don't believe it.
Silk Lady 2:	We can help you avoid the Sadnap.
Aw Boo:	*(suspicious)* Don't need your help.
Hua:	But –
Aw Boo:	Come along.

Aw Boo and Hua pull the wagon. Threatening music is played by the Stage Manager. Transition from light to darkness.

Suddenly from the shadows comes a large puppet Monster with a ferocious worm-like head. The Monster can be manipulated by the Narrators 1 and 2 with long sticks. The Monster swoops in and around Aw Boo and Hua. They are terrified and try to avoid it. Music continues under the scene.

Hua:	We should have listened to the women.
Aw Boo:	Don't think of that now. We must get out of here.

The Monster makes another attack, swooping near them and driving Hua and Aw Boo from the bamboo forest. Hua starts to run.

Aw Boo:	The wagon. Don't forget the wagon.
	Hua and Aw Boo quickly pull the wagon out of the bamboo forest before the Monster catches them again.
Hua:	*(still terrified)* We will never make it through the forest without the help of the women.
Aw Boo:	And we need to go through the forest to reach Dazu.
	The Silk Ladies enter and continue their silk ritual. Hua approaches them.
Silk Lady 1:	You are still here?
Hua:	The beast chased us from the forest.
Aw Boo:	Can you help us?
Silk Lady 2:	*(as she works)* You gave us jade before.
Hua:	For your silk.
Silk Lady 1:	We liked the jade you gave us so much –
Silk Lady 2:	We want more.
Aw Boo:	We will trade you for your silk.
Silk Lady 1:	We will trade our help for your jade.
Aw Boo:	What do you mean?
Silk Lady 2:	We will help you through the bamboo forests.
Hua:	And the wild Sadnap?
Silk Lady 1:	We know how to protect you from the beast.
Silk Lady 2:	But we want your jade…all your jade…in return.
Aw Boo:	But you can't take it all. That jade is precious.
Hua:	You gave us silk for one piece of the jade.
Silk Lady 1:	Are not your lives worth more than silk?
	The Silk Ladies start to walk away from Aw Boo and Hua.
Aw Boo:	We will give you our jade!
	Aw Boo and Hua start to walk in place pulling the now half-filled wagon. The Silk Ladies walk in front.
Hua:	How will you protect us from the beast?
Silk Lady 1:	The Sadnap is part silk worm and part panda. We will enchant him with our song.

Starts to sing.

Silk Lady 2: When the Sadnap hears the song, he will not harm you –

Joins in the song.

The Two Silk Ladies sing the "Song of Enchantment" as Hua and Aw Boo pull the wagon through the bamboo forest. Lights come up on Hua and Aw Boo, who have been led safely through the forest.

Hua: Where are we?

Silk Lady 1: Follow this road to the large river.

Silk Ladies start to exit.

Silk Lady 2: And thank you for the jade.

They exit.

Hua: *(pulling)* The wagon is easier to pull now.

Aw Boo: *(hits Hua with a burlap sack)* That is because we have lost most of our treasures.

Hua: But we will bring the rest back to Dazu.

Aw Boo: *(looks under the cloth on wagon)* There is still enough to make us wealthy.

Narrator 1 pulls back the screen indicating the river scene. Narrator 2 puts on the mask of the Ferryman.

Hua: All we have to do is cross the river.

Ferryman: *(greets them)* Hello! You have survived your journey to the North.

Aw Boo: *(bitterly)* Yes.

Ferryman: And did you find more jade?

Hua: No. We even lost –

Aw Boo: *(to Hua)* Silence!

To Ferryman.

We need to take your ferry.

Hua: You brought us across the river for three Yuan.

Ferryman: But the waters are too high. The monsoon rains have made the river too dangerous to cross.

Aw Boo: But we need to reach Dazu!

Ferryman:	You must wait.
Hua:	How long?
Ferryman:	Five months.
Aw Boo:	We cannot wait that long.
Ferryman:	You have no choice.
Aw Boo:	Can anyone take us across the river?
Ferryman:	I am the only Ferryman who can. I know the river like my own family.
Aw Boo:	Then six Yuan. We will double your price.
Ferryman:	*(incredulous)* Six Yuan?
Aw Boo:	*(laughs weakly)* And we still do not have a horse.
Hua:	We had one but –
Aw Boo:	*(to Hua)* Silence!
	To Ferryman.
	Will you take us?
Ferryman:	For my price. Not yours.
Aw Boo:	What is your price?
Ferryman:	I am trading my talents of many years to navigate this river.
Aw Boo:	Yes?
Ferryman:	I need a wagon.
Aw Boo:	Our wagon!
Ferryman	I risk my boat for you. You must give up your wagon for me.
Aw Boo:	No!
Ferryman:	Then wait here until the water is down.
Hua:	*(quietly)* We have no choice.
Aw Boo:	*(nearly chokes on the words)* Take the wagon.
	Aw Boo and Hua each take a sack of treasures from the wagon. The wagon is now empty.
Aw Boo:	*(bitterly)* There. Now take us across the river.
	The Ferryman rolls out the bamboo mat. Narrator 1 helps in the process. The Ferryman takes long bamboo pole and starts to push the boat away from the shore.

Hua:	Wait for us!

Hua and Aw Boo, each holding an armful of treasures, scramble on board the boat. The Ferryman pushes the boat further out into the river. Music accompanies the trip across the river.

Ferryman:	See how I miss the dangerous rocks. No other Ferryman knows this river as I do.
Hua:	*(impressed)* Yes. You will bring us safely to the other side.

Ferryman stops his motion with the bamboo stick.

Aw Boo:	Why have you stopped?

Ferryman does not speak.

We are only halfway across.

Ferryman:	My arrangement was to take you both across the river.
Aw Boo:	Yes. And for that we traded our wagon.
Ferryman:	*(points to bundles and sacks that Aw Boo and Hua are holding)* Then you must throw those sacks in the water.
Aw Boo:	We can't do that!
Ferryman:	Then I go no further.
Aw Boo:	These are all we have left.
Hua:	Yes.
Ferryman:	I agreed to take you over – not your sacks.
Aw Boo:	But I assumed.
Ferryman:	Assume nothing on a dangerous river. Your sacks in the water.
Hua:	What do you want to transport our treasures, too?
Ferryman:	Your friend's cloak.
Aw Boo:	*(pulls it tighter around him., on the verge of tears)* Not my cloak.
Hua:	Take mine.

Starts to take it off.

Ferryman:	I don't want a cloak of rags. His cloak I want. Furs and jewels.
Hua:	But mine will keep you as warm.
Ferryman:	So?

Aw Boo shakes his head vehemently.

Then your sacks must go overboard.

Ferryman starts to pull the sack from Aw Boo. A brief struggle before Aw Boo finally gives in.

Aw Boo gives Ferryman his cloak. The Ferryman puts the cloak around him and resumes rowing to the other side of the river. Music underscores this transaction and the rest of the journey.

The other side of the river is reached. Narrator 1 rolls up the bamboo mat. Narrator 2 takes off mask of the Ferryman.

Aw Boo and Hua are lying against their sacks. They are exhausted. Aw Boo opens his eyes. He is shaking from the cold and the lack of a cloak. He has been feigning sleep and quietly pulls off Hua's cloak of rags and puts it around him. Aw Boo takes the two sacks and runs off.

Hua wakes up. He realizes that his cloak has been taken. He sees the sacks are gone.

Hua: *(runs off, calling after Aw Boo)* Aw Boo, you should have listened to me! We should have turned back when we still had something.

Exits on the run.

Narrator 2:   Aw Boo wanted to reach Dazu before Hua. So he could sell the treasures that remained in the two sacks. But Aw Boo, in his haste, found himself on a narrow mountain path. A heavy mist kept him from seeing where he was going.

Narrator 2 ties black silk over Aw Boo's eyes. Narrator 1 pulls back screen revealing mountain pass.

One false step and Aw Boo would fall thousands of feet to the valley below.

Aw Boo: Help me! I cannot see. The mist is so thick.

Narrator 1 has put on the mask of the Lady Who Picks Tea. She is carrying a lantern.

Aw Boo: I see a light.

Lady: Over here.

Aw Boo: Who are you?

Lady: I traded tea with you for one hundred Yuan.

Aw Boo: Yes. Yes. Will you help me now?

Lady: I live near here. I know these mountain paths.

Aw Boo:	Will you lead me to safety?
Lady:	I will trade my knowledge of these mountains.
Aw Boo:	*(desperate)* Yes.
Lady:	And the light from my lantern.
Aw Boo:	Anything.
Lady:	For your two sacks.
Aw Boo:	But you don't know what is in them.
Lady:	No.
Aw Boo:	Nothing of value.
Lady:	If there was nothing of value, you would not risk your life carrying them.

> *Starts to walk away.*

Aw Boo:	Where are you going?
Lady:	You do not want my help.
Aw Boo:	*(desperate)* Take the sacks!

> *Lady puts them on her shoulder.*

But lead me out of here.

> *Lady takes Aw Boo's hand and leads him off. Music underscores the scene.*
>
> *Narrator 2 pulls back the screen revealing the outskirts of Dazu.*
>
> *Aw Boo is ashamed to return to the city poor and in rags. He is lying by the side of the road. The sound of a wagon startles him. The wagon, dressed slightly differently than Aw Boo's, appears. The wagon is pulled by an actor (formerly Hua) as the Horse and led by two wealthy merchants (played by Narrators 1 and 2) wearing masks.*

Merchant 1:	*(to Aw Boo)* Who are you, poor fellow?
Aw Boo:	A merchant.
Merchant 2:	*(laughing)* A merchant? You are a beggar.
Merchant 1:	Give him some rice.
Merchant 2:	*(stopping Merchant 1)* No. If he is a merchant, let him trade with us.

> *To Aw Boo.*

	Do you have anything to trade for this rice?
Aw Boo:	*(looks hungrily at the bowl of rice.,wanting it)* My cloak.
Merchant 1:	Who would want those rags?
Aw Boo:	For your horse. To keep the flies off him.
Merchant 2:	Good trade! For that, here is your rice.
Aw Boo:	*(takes the rice, and puts the cloak on the horse, begins to eat eagerly from the rice bowl, speaking between bites)* Where are you going?
Merchant 2:	*(laughs cynically)* Somewhere you will never see, beggar! We are going across the Yangtze River, through the bamboo forests to the Great Wall and on to the Gobi desert.
Merchant 1:	*(cynically)* We'd ask you to come. But we have no room for you in our wagon.

> *Both Merchants laugh.*

We are going to fill our wagon with the treasures of the North.

> *Starts to beat the drum..*

Merchant 1 & 2: *(sing or chant)* We are from the city. We are wise.
We will travel to the small towns and villages.
We will buy the treasures from the people we meet.
We will pay them very little money.
Because they do not know their true value.
But we are from the city and we are wise.
We will fill our wagon with tea and silk and jade.

> *Aw Boo watches as the Horse pulls wagon off the stage led by the Merchants 1 and 2. Aw Boo takes the wrinkled map from under his shirt. He starts to offer it to the Merchants.*

Aw Boo:	I have something else to trade.

> *They do not hear him. Aw Boo starts to run after them.*

Wait!

> *Changes his mind and holds up his map in defiance.*

Why should I give you my map? Find out yourselves the way to the North!

> *Aw Boo runs from the area. He holds map tightly.*

> *Narrators 1 and 2 take off the masks of the Merchants. They meet in the centre of the stage.*

Narrator 1:	Wagons will continue to travel north.

Narrator 2:   Will they ever learn from the Merchants of Dazu?

Hua and Aw Boo enter dressed as at the beginning of the play.

They now represent the Actors playing the roles of the merchants rather than the characters. They both pull the empty wagon. Narrators 1 and 2 accompany the Merchants on the various instruments.

Merchant 1 & 2: *(final chant)* A Wagon empty. A wagon full.
Greed takes us further than we should.
Sand and water. Rock and Wood.
We cannot see what is in front of our nose.
A wagon full. A wagon empty.
A journey into another time, another place.
Our tale is finished.
Thank you for your eyes and ears.

The Company bows.

The End

Screen for Merchants of Dazu
Have a long, continuously painted screen of travels suspended from a 1/4 inch steel cable that could pull one way from behind the flats to show the first part of the journey and be pulled back the other way to show the return portion of the journey

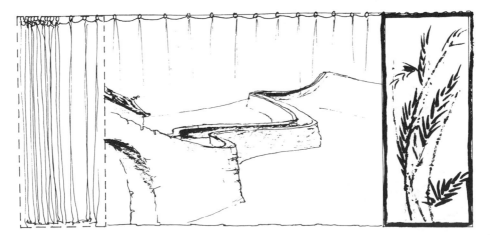

Prairie Dragons
SHARON POLLOCK

Design Concept by Douglas McCullough

SHARON POLLOCK is one of Canada's most respected and widely produced playwrights. Among her many plays are *Blood Relations* and *Doc,* both winners of the Governor General's Award, *Sweet Land of Liberty,* which received a Nellie Award for Best Radio Drama, and *The Person's Case,* which received a Golden Sheaf Award for Human Drama, Television. Among her many other honours are the Chalmers Award, the Writers Guild of Alberta Award of Excellence, the Alberta Award of Excellence and the Canadian Australian Literary Prize. Sharon Pollock is currently Artistic Director of Theatre New Brunswick.

Prairie Dragons was first performed by Quest Theatre, Calgary, Alberta, in October, 1987, with the following cast:

Andy Curtis
Jan Derbyshire
Marianne Moroney
Chris Youngren

Directed by Duval Lang
Designed by Linda Leon

PLAYWRIGHT'S NOTE

A play for four actors; could be four women; must include two women, one consistently playing Lily Kwong, a girl of 12 years, and the other playing Sarah Whitherspoon, a girl of 16 years.

We see the Stage Manager; s/he is always visible ringing bells, banging cymbals, beating drums, operating the equipment which provides sound or music cues when required. S/he moves the life-size figures (to be described later) pushing them forward, moving them back, as required. S/he passes actors such small or large items of apparel they don when they play or become a character. Sarah and Lily need no such assistance. They are the only two characters whose costuming and appearance are complete as the characters.

The Four Actors and the Stage Manager are individual manifestations of one entity, the Prairie Dragon who tells the tale. With the exception of the Stage Manager, they share the dialogue of the Prairie Dragon although one voice (not that of the actors playing either Lily or Sarah) may predominate. Any combination of the four, or only one, may "operate" the Dragon at any time.

The dialogue of the Dragon has not been divided into the various voices. I leave that to the Director and rehearsal process. Stage directions are not complete and are merely indicators of half-formed ideas in the mind of the playwright. The hope or intent is that they may be catalytic or helpful in our discovery of the "way of telling" and/or the style of the piece.

Sound/music always accompanies Dragon.

Prairie Dragons

*The life-size cutout figures of the characters pushed forward by
Stage Manager: the characters of Lily and Sarah are complete
replicas of the cut-out figures of Lily and Sarah. Other figures
include Mr. Whitherspoon, 55 years old, dressed for work on the
homestead; Johnny Whitherspoon in a W.W. I uniform leaning
on his rifle and reading a letter; a gravestone on which is
engraved:*

> *Amelia Emily Whitherspoon*
> *Born December 12, 1880*
> *Died December 12, 1904*
> *"Called home";*

*Mr. Lowe, a banker in a suit and a moustache; Mr. Kwong,
Lily's father, wearing his restaurant attire; Sam Kwong, Lily's
brother, 15 years old and a student; Mrs. Kwong, Lily's mother,
who is bent over a washtub and scrub board. Each figure is
mounted on a base which enables it to be moved much as a
croupier moves a stack of chips, or as life-size chess figures are
moved on a playing field by eccentric British twit gamesmen.*

*Behind each figure (with the exception of Lily and Sarah) is a
pole around which is draped, hung, placed, the minimal prop
and/or costume pieces which are offered by the Stage Manager to
the actor when s/he is about to play that character. For instance,
when a scene between Lily and her Father is about to take place,
I see the figure of Lily's Father being pushed forward. The actor
who will play Lily's Father steps in front of that figure ,staring
into its eyes as if being charged by gazing into a full-length
mirror reflecting an image of her/himself. As s/he assumes the
stance of the figure, s/he dons the apron, skullcap with pigtail
attached, takes the pencil and restaurant order pad, all offered
by the Stage Manager, and steps into the scene with Lily.*

*No one plays Mrs. Kwong. Although Lily may speak to her cut-
out figure, Mrs. Kwong remains frozen at work at the washtub.
Similarly, Sarah may speak to the gravestone of her Mother.*

*As the Dragon describes characters, only the cutout figures are
pushed forward (no actors assume characters).*

*A gorgeous Dragon whose colours are predominantly orange
and red lies in a state of collapse.*

The sound of tinkling bells or chimes.

The head of the Dragon moves, rises.

Dragon: A Dragon Tale.
                Tale of a Dragon!

The Stage Manager appears from under the Dragon. S/he carries the bells or chimes. As the Dragon continues its dialogue, the Stage Manager will unroll orange paper or material "drapes" so they cover the doors of the auditorium or playing space. All windows or accesses to the outside world should be similarly covered by these orange "drapes." They are good luck seals. The Stage Manager will operate such sound, music and lights as are deemed necessary for the Dragon's speech and dance.

As the Dragon moves and speaks as an entity (sometimes with one, sometimes more than one voice), any of the four actors may appear from under it, speaking and moving. It's as if the Dragon is in a constant state of separating and coalescing.

Dragon
Transformer
Dragon
Magician
Giver of laws
And the art of painting
What?
        The Art of Painting!
Oh.
Benevolent, beautiful
Friendly and wise
Head
        like a camel
Ear
        like a cow
Neck
        like a snake
Belly
        of frog
Scales
        of carp
Eagle claws
Tiger paws
Tail tail tail
Tail of a dragon
Sail thro' the sky breathing clouds
Burrow thro' earth leaving paths
with a pearl
pearl for power

pearl, yes, here
under the chin pearly pearl
and purple
Purple?
Whiskers of purple three feet long
spelling death for mosquitoes and flies.
Anyone for a whisker, guys, girls,
adults of indeterminate age hear
the tale of a dragon
   Here the tail of a dragon?
Here the Tale of a Dragon.
A story?
   Yes. Narrative?
Yarn. Fable? Account
of what might have been
never could be!
probably was
in the village of Roundridge?
   yes, call it that
province of Alta?
   yes, call it that
country of Cannon?
   yes, call it that
as told by a dragon?
   You're calling it that?
Prairie Dragon.
   We're calling it that.
Roundridge
   to the west land rises
Steep? Yes. Bumps?
Mountainous humps
   to the east stand on a box
see straight to the end of the earth.
   Don't fall off
   box?
   earth!
North catch glint of the sun on ice
south air rises in slow undulating waves of heat
   undulating what?
   pulsing rippling
   waviness waves of heat
and over
the big blue bowl
   under
   under?
under the underground paths of Dragons.

Prairie Dragons
telling the what of the whom
as in cast of characters just for a start
George John Franklin Adamson Daniel Whitherspoon
husband of Amelia Em
deceased
  in the year of the Dragon 1904
  born and died on the 12th day of the
  12th month in a
     12th year
  a year of the Dragon
Mother of Matthew George Everett John Franklin
Stephen Adamson Robb
  usually known as Ronnie
and presently serving in France
  World War One
a son to be proud of –
  did we mention Sarah?
Mother of Sarah
Mr. Lowe lower than low
friend of the family
listen to Lowe, he'll help you Sarah
  Hah!
Mr. Kwong, hard-working entrepreneur
one who undertakes to establish and run
underground dragon paths
No!
to establish and run
"Mr. Kwong's Roundridge Restaurant and Laundry"
Ah, yes, Mr. Kwong
  husband of Mrs.
Who?
Mrs. Kwong, mother of Sam
quick and smart as a whip
Oh, Sam will go places, Sam
  and Lily
  Lillian.
  Lily
born in the year of the Dragon
December 12th, 1904.
This year today the time of the tale?
  Time of the tail?
  Story.
  Narrative?
  Yarn.
  Shush!

1916   Year of the Dragon!
        it comes in 12's
        Shush!
        it's funny how things fit together
        Shush!
Lily's 12th year
and Sarah
        1916 in Roundridge.
Drought
dry
dust in the back of your throat
itchy eyes from the arid air
grass whithers and burns
crops struggle
the head of the wheat shrinks
lightning thunder
to the east to the west
but rain never falls here
look for rain
pray for rain
the heat sits heavy like death
and
George John Franklin Adamson Daniel Whitherspoon

> *Sarah, looking identical to the cutout figure (these figures will be referred to as mirror figures), stands in front of her mirror figure looking into its eyes. She wears a pearl on a chain.*

Father of Sarah rides out to check on his men
his crops
and the new barn whose foundations he's dug
        Take Care
His horse is black
        Watch Out
Its foot strikes the edge of a gopher hole.

> *The Stage Manager deals the mirror figure of Mr. Whitherspoon a blow with a long stick, and the figure falls over.*

Sarah: *(turns and screams)* Papa!!!

> *Sarah approaches her Mother's gravestone. She carries two pieces of wood and some binder twine.*

Sarah: Guess who, Mama?...It's me, it's Sarah. What on earth do you think people would say if they could see me up here talkin' to a gravestone? "That Sarah Whitherspoon's gone right silly – silly Sarah Whitherspoon!" But you can hear me, can't you?

I've been comin' up here for how long? Ever since I was four and I'm gonna keep right on 'cause it helps...I guess you know about Papa? People been real nice since he died, and soon as Ronnie comes home we'll see Papa gets a stone right beside you and just as nice. Do you think this wooden one'll do till then? ...Sometimes I get scared thinkin' a things, but you know what I do? I just put my hand round your gold necklace with the little pearl that I never take off, and that helps. Or I come up here for a talk. Things'll be fine, Mama, I mean I'm sixteen years old. You were married at sixteen and havin' babies at seventeen. If you could do that, I guess I can look after things here till Ronnie gets home. I think I can...Do you think I can, Mama?

Mr. Lowe: Miss Whitherspoon?

Sarah: There.

> *The two pieces of wood are tied together forming a cross.*

Mr. Lowe: Miss Whitherspoon!

Sarah: Do you think it'll stay if I just –

Mr. Lowe: Sarah!

Sarah: Oh,

> *She puts down the cross and moves away from the gravestone to meet Mr. Lowe.*

coming!

> *Whispers.*

I'll be back.

Good mornin', Mr. Lowe. I was just up on the hill scannin' the sky for rain clouds.

Mr. Lowe: No rain in that sky.

Sarah: I didn't hear you ride in.

Mr. Lowe: I left the carriage down by the new barn your Papa was buildin'.

Sarah: It's goin' to be a beautiful barn all right.

Mr. Lowe: I hear the foundation wall fell in.

Sarah: I got a man out from town workin' on that.

Mr. Lowe: That's a waste a good money, Miss Sarah.

Sarah:	I don't think so.
Mr. Lowe:	But how's a young girl to know these things, eh?
Sarah:	I know Papa wanted that barn finished, so I'm gonna finish that barn. Can I offer you tea or a nice cold drink, Mr. Lowe?
Mr. Lowe:	It's not a social call, Miss Sarah.

Stage Manager holds tray with once fine but now cracked tea service on it. Sarah pours tea.

Sarah:	Mama brought this tea set out from the old country. Two cups are gone beyond repair, but the rest are still good.
Mr. Lowe:	It's a business call.
Sarah:	What kind a business?
Mr. Lowe:	You're alone here, Miss Sarah, with your Papa gone and Mama long gone, and brother Ronnie away at the War.
Sarah:	There's the four farm hands and the bunkhouse cook and me, I don't call that livin' alone.
Mr. Lowe:	No family. No man runnin' things till your brother gets back.
Sarah:	I'm runnin' things till my brother gets back.
Mr. Lowe:	And a bank payment comin' up at the end a the season.
Sarah:	There's a good lot a money in Papa's account. I should know. I've been keepin' account a the money for the last two years. What exactly are you tryin' to say, Mr. Lowe?
Mr. Lowe:	You may have money now, but if no rain comes and your crop dies off, what will you have come the end a the season, eh?… I'm thinkin' a you and your brother, Miss Sarah.
Sarah:	You are, are you?
Mr. Lowe:	Best thing for you and your brother is to sell this place. I'd give you a real good price.
Sarah:	You would, would you?
Mr. Lowe:	I sure would. You put that in the bank. A nice nest egg for when your brother gets back, and you, you could move into town, board with Mrs. Lowe and me. What do you think?
Sarah:	I'm not so much thinkin' as rememberin' you comin' to Papa last year askin' to buy, and Papa tellin' you to go jump in a slough.
Mr. Lowe:	Your Papa's gone now, and there ain't nobody here to look after the place.

Sarah:	Aren't you forgettin'? There's me and four farmhands and the bunkhouse cook.
Mr. Lowe:	Nobody in charge.
Sarah:	I am in charge, Mr. Lowe.

Strange sound.

Voice Off:	That foundation wall fell in agin!
Sarah:	Well shore it up! Put some bracin' in this time!
Mr. Lowe:	A girl can't run a place like this.
Sarah:	Wanna bet?
Mr. Lowe:	It ain't gonna rain.
Sarah:	Is so.
Mr. Lowe:	And the crop's gonna die.
Sarah:	Is not.
Mr. Lowe:	There'll be no money left at the end a the season.
Sarah:	Will so.
Mr. Lowe:	And your brother'll come home to nothin'.
Sarah:	Will not.
Mr. Lowe:	And it'll all be your fault, Miss Sarah!
Dragon:	Whose fault, Miss Sarah!
Sarah:	Oh,

She drops a tea cup.

I've...I've cracked Mama's cup. I've cracked Mama's cup.

Dragon:	Crack!

Lightning splits the sky.

Dragon:	No rain here.
Sarah:	Mama?
Dragon:	Mama

Dragons
Mama Dragons lay eggs like beautiful stones
Beautiful stones like hen-size eggs
left alone by a mountain stream
Mama Dragons lay eggs to the number of nine
Crack

lightning splits the egg
nine eggs split
nine tiny dragons float up to the sky
up uup uuup
        except this one who hides in the seam
        of a coat
        except this one who...

Stage Manager rolls a hen-size beautiful stone towards Lily who is carrying a basket of laundry. The egg comes to rest near Lily, who puts the basket down and picks up the egg. The basket has a large lettered sign saying "Whitherspoons" pinned to it. Lily carries a dictionary as well.

Lily: It's beautiful...It catches the light...smooth, smooth as the skin on the inside of a baby's arm...Inside...inside, a tiny shadow... It's warm, from the sun do you think? I'm taking it home.

She puts the egg in a pocket, picks up the basket and continues on her way to Whitherspoons.

I'll place it on the old wooden table that's pitted and scarred, I'll push the table under the window, and I'll draw my stone, the table and window on the back of a brown paper bag with my pencil.

She has approached Sarah and Mr. Lowe.

Mr. Lowe: I come out here to do you a favour.

Sarah: I don't need any favours from you.

Mr. Lowe: You'll be wishin' you accepted my offer 'cause things are gonna go right down hill, I can tell you that.

Sarah: I rode horse with my Papa since I was four, I worked in the fields, built fence, helped the bunkhouse cook and kept Papa's accounts for the last two years. And I say the Whitherspoon farm is gonna grow and prosper. When Ronnie comes home –

Mr. Lowe: If Ronnie comes home.

Sarah: Don't say that!

Mr. Lowe: It's a war. Young men get killed in a war.

Lily: I brought your laundry, Miss Sarah.

Sarah: You get off a this farm, and don't you ever come back.

Mr. Lowe: You'll be invitin' me back end a the season.

Sarah: Go!

Mr. Lowe:	And I'll offer you half a what I'm offerin' you now!
Sarah:	Pass me that gun, Lily.

Lily takes a rifle from the Stage Manager and passes it to Sarah.

Mr. Lowe:	A girl runnin' a farm goes against nature.
Sarah:	I'm warnin' you.
Mr. Lowe:	Drought'll get you! Then you'll come beggin' to sell!

Sarah fires a shot.

Mr. Lowe:	OHHEE!

Sarah fires a second shot.

Lily:	Look at him run!
Sarah:	Like a speck a water on a hot griddle.
Lily:	Good-bye, Mr. Lowe!
Sarah:	Nice a you to drop in!…

They're laughing.

Oh, my…do you…do you think I should a done that?

Lily:	Well…
Sarah:	I shouldn't a done that.
Lily:	I shouldn't a passed it to you.
Sarah:	Didn't solve a thing…but when he said that about Ronnie not comin' back I just got so darn mad…Do you think a girl runnin' a farm goes against nature, Lily?

Strange sound.

Voice Off:	The bracin' in the foundation wall fell in!
Sarah:	Well brace it agin with timber!
Voice Off:	Got a letter here for the Kwongs. Yes siree, a letter addressed to who? "Care of Kwong's Roundridge Restaurant and Laundry!" Mr. Kwong.

Stage Manager passes Mr. Kwong a letter which Mr. Kwong opens.

Mr. Kwong:	Who would be sending a letter to me? Most unusual.

Reading the letter, the letter is saying:

Voice Off:	(*snotty English accent*) Dear Miss Kwong.

Mr. Kwong:	Miss Kwong?
	Looks at the envelope.
Voice Off:	The Cannonian Institute of Uniform English Spelling is pleased to inform you that your application for inclusion in the National Spell-Off has been accepted.
Mr. Kwong:	This letter is addressed to Lily.
Voice Off:	*(as Lily approaches and Mr. Kwong peruses the letter)* Kindly present yourself with other competitors at Beggtowne Civic Auditorium at 12 noon, August 24th, 1916. Yours truly.
Lily:	It's a spelling bee, Father.
Mr. Kwong:	I understand that.
Lily:	With a twenty-five dollar prize for the best speller.
Mr. Kwong:	I understand that.
Lily:	I am a very good speller, Father.
Mr. Kwong:	What I don't understand is why you have entered this competition without asking permission.
Lily:	I was afraid you'd say no.
Mr. Kwong:	Why do you want to do this?
Lily:	I'm a good speller. Last Regional Bee I won every age group.
Mr. Kwong:	No.
Lily:	Why not?
Mr. Kwong:	No, this thing you can't do.
Lily:	I want to know why.
Mr. Kwong:	It has no purpose, Lily.
Lily:	A twenty-five dollar prize, Father.
Mr. Kwong:	Oh...Oh. Perhaps Sam could enter this contest. Sam!
Lily:	Sam is a terrible speller!
Mr. Kwong:	You are right, Lily – but a twenty-five dollar prize. This would be a grand addition to Sam's education fund.
Lily:	That wasn't...
Mr. Kwong:	You were saying?
Lily:	The prize money, Father, I would –

Mr. Kwong:	You know, all extra money earned by the family goes towards Sam's education.
Lily:	But –
Mr. Kwong:	That is the way it is, Lily.
Lily:	I would –
Mr. Kwong:	What?
Lily:	I would pay, from my very own money, the prize money –
Mr. Kwong:	But there is no "very own money," all money belongs to the family.
Lily:	I would pay for brushes and paints and paper and lessons in watercolours from –
Mr. Kwong:	Stop!
Lily:	I'm going to be an artist when I grow up, Father, I'm going to paint, you know how well I draw, Father!
Mr. Kwong:	Stop, Lily! Now – soon you will leave school, you will help in the laundry, you will marry. That is your contribution to the success of the family. That way happiness lies.
Lily:	I –
Mr. Kwong:	Respect and listen. Obey.

Mr. Kwong rips up the letter and retreats.

Sam:	It's for the best, Lily.
Lily:	Best for who?
Sam:	The family stands together, what is best for all is best for one.
Lily:	On August 24th I'm going to be in that Civic Auditorium and I'll win, you wait and see.
Sam:	You'll do what Father says – you wait and see.
Lily:	Why can't I enter the contest and spend the money I win however I want?
Sam:	Can you remember coming to Roundridge, Lily?
Lily:	Answer the question.
Sam:	Do you remember the city?
Lily:	I am so tried of hearing this old story.
Sam:	You were only a baby and I wasn't much bigger, and Father

and uncle hid Mother and us in the yard at the back. The people broke all the windows and they stole all the goods and they burnt down the stores. So the merchant Kwong brought his family here, for the city was no longer safe for his family.

Lily: And what's that got to do with the spelling bee, please?

Sam: We're different, Lily, and people are afraid of the difference.

Lily: That isn't an answer.

Sam: Maybe some day things will change, but till then each of us has a job to do. My job is to get a good education, to work hard for the family and the community and to obey Father who is older and wiser. Your job is to marry and have children, to listen and to obey, not to be dreaming and drawing and spelling.

Lily: Do you think I draw well?

Sam: You never listen, Lily.

Lily: I do so listen. I just don't agree!

She looks to the figure of Mrs. Kwong.

Lily: What do you think, Mother?

You work so hard...do times change?...Father can't draw...nor Sam...When you were a girl did you want to draw?... Mother? ...tell me the way you think happiness lies?...Mother?

Sarah and Ronnie each with a letter.

Ronnie: Dear Sarah...

Sarah: Dear Sarah...

Ronnie & Sarah:
                We're moving up to the front tomorrow so I'll –

Ronnie: Try and get this off in the mail bag tonight. It's hard to believe that Mr. Lowe has acted so abominably towards you, but I must confess that the thought of you running things has given me cause for some concern as well.

Sarah: It has?

Ronnie: I'm not so sure that continuing with the farm is what I really want to do when I get back.

Sarah: What?

Ronnie: It's possible I might move to the city –

Sarah: Ronnie?!

Ronnie:	And take up some other vocation.
Sarah:	What "vocation"?
Lily:	*(spells)* V-O-C-A-T-I-O-N

With open dictionary.

Ronnie:	Of course, you would make your home with me until you married and –
Sarah:	I don't believe it. I think he's lost his mind.
Lily:	*(passes Sarah the dictionary)* It's probably the war.
Sarah:	I hope so. Abbacy.
Lily:	A-B-B-A-C-Y.
Sarah:	Papa cleared the land, Mama's gravestone is here and the wooden cross for Papa – how can he talk about movin' to the city and the rest of all that? Abbreviate.
Lily:	A-B-B…
Mr. Lowe:	What did I tell you, Miss Sarah?
Sarah:	You again.
Lily:	R-E-V…
Mr. Lowe:	Hot enough for you?
Lily:	I-A…
Mr. Lowe:	Dry enough for you?
Lily:	T-E.
Mr. Lowe:	Look at that sky?
Sarah:	Abdicate.
Mr. Lowe:	No rain in that sky.
Lily:	A-B-D-I-C-A-T-E.
Mr. Lowe:	Would you like to talk price, Miss Sarah?
Sarah:	My brother may not be plannin' on farmin'.
Mr. Lowe:	'ppears not.
Sarah:	So there's no need a my takin' charge a things for him.
Mr. Lowe:	That's right.
Sarah:	So I've decided to take charge a things for me.

Mr. Lowe:	Meanin'?
Sarah:	Meanin' if my brother's not gonna farm, it doesn't matter a bit, 'cause I'm gonna farm. I'm not doin' it for him, I'm doin' it for me.
Mr. Lowe:	I've never heard a no female farmer.
Sarah:	Then you must be deaf 'cause I just told you a one. Me!
Mr. Lowe:	Women workin' the land turns the whole world topsy turvey. That's why we got this drought! Entire countryside is gonna turn dark brown and crisp as burnt toast, and it's all your fault!
Sarah:	Get!
Mr. Lowe:	Supposin' it does rain – with no barn that crop's gonna rot in the field!
Sarah:	Go!
Mr. Lowe:	I'm goin'.
Sarah:	Abdomen.
Lily:	A-B –
Sarah:	I'm not thin, and I'm not pretty. I got hair like wire, and I'm taller than most every boy I knew goin' to school. Feel that muscle, Lily.
Lily:	(does so as she spells) M-U-S-C-L-E.
Sarah:	I can do as good a day's work as most anyone my age.
Lily:	A-G-E.
Sarah:	And I got a good head for figures. If I like what I'm doin', can it really be wrong?
Lily:	W-R-O-N-G!
Sarah:	If you want to go to that spellin' bee on the 24th a August, I'll take you there in the buggy.
Lily:	Would you?! Oh, Sarah! That would be…that would be… wrong. I just can't do it. Not unless Father says yes.
Sarah:	How likely is that?
Lily:	Not very likely.
Sarah:	Abduct?
Lily:	But I can still hope. A-B-D-U-C-T!
Sarah:	Do you think I'm goin' against nature and that's what's causin'

this drought?

Strange sound.

Voice Off:	Foundation, bracin' and timber fell in agin!
Sarah:	And I can't even get the foundation dug for that barn, much less raise walls and a roof. Could it all be my fault?
Lily:	According to Sam it's probably my fault.

She takes the round stone egg out of her pocket.

I have caused disharmony in our family by being selfish and willful. When I cook the rice it's always sticky, and the drought means no one has any money to eat at the restaurant.

Sarah:	Aberrant.
Lily:	A-B-E-R-R...Do you think we're aberrant, Sarah?
Sarah:	I don't even know what it means...

She reads from the dictionary.

Lily:	A-N-T.
Sarah:	"To vary from normal, to stray...
Dragon:	*(voice joins Sarah's)* from the usual course."
Lily:	C-O-U-R-S-E.
Sarah:	Did you hear that?
Lily:	What?
Sarah:	Nothing – "Partial mental...
Dragon:	*(voice joins Sarah's)* derangement.
Lily:	D-E-R-A-N-G-E-M-E-N-T.

Sarah hears the Dragon but can't believe her ears. Lily is unaware of the Dragon's voice.

Sarah:	Lily.
Lily:	Go on.
Dragon:	Did you know Mr. Lowe is calling you?
Sarah:	Barmie.
Lily:	B-A-R-M-I-E.
Sarah:	Lily!
Lily:	Was that wrong?

Sarah:	No, it was…Never mind. Cantank…
Dragon:	*(voice joins Sarah's)* tankerous.

As Lily spells "cantankerous."

Sarah:	Lily!
Lily:	What?
Dragon:	"Demented and bent. Eccentric and odd."
Sarah:	Listen…
Dragon:	"Factious and fake." Ooooohhhhh.
Lily:	There's a bit of a wind.
Dragon:	"And she's only a miss."

Sarah sees the Dragon, Lily does not.

Sarah:	Look!
Lily:	Where?
Dragon:	She keeps on like this, what will she be when she's old?
Sarah:	There!

Dragon:	"A crone
	        a harridan
	                hag."

Sarah:	There!
Lily:	Where?
Dragon:	"Commonly known as witch!"
Lily:	What did you see?
Sarah:	Head like a camel, ear like a cow, neck like a snake, frog belly, carp scales, eagle claws, tiger paws…
Lily:	You saw a dragon, Sarah!
Sarah:	There aren't no dragons in Roundridge!
Lily:	Then, what did you see?
Sarah:	I saw…
Dragon:	*(slowly reveals itself to Lily and Sarah, preening itself, thinking itself beautiful)* Head like camel, ear like cow, neck like snake, belly like frog, scales like carp, eagle claws, tiger paws.
Lily:	This is either very good –
Sarah:	Or very bad.

Dragon: And pearlpalepearl
               pearly pearl round
               for power.

Lily: Like your pearl, Sarah!

Sarah: My Mother's pearl.

Lily: *(the Dragon indicates the gravestone)* Born and died on the 12th
               day of the 12th month of a Dragon year!

Dragon: Hear hear of the birth of dragons
                       split egg dragons numbering nine
               First sounds like a bell
               Second a harp
               Third is thirsty
                       always thirsty
               Fourth is a climber
               Fifth is a fighter
               Sixth is a scholar
               The ears of seven can hear a pin drop on a feather bed.

Lily: Eight?

Dragon: Just sits around.

Sarah: Nine?

Dragon: Lifter of weights.

                       Holds up weights.

               Mark its image?

Lily: On foundation walls?

Dragon: Thirsty one?

Lily: Carve on cups?

Dragon: Scholar dragon?

Lily: Paint on books.

Sarah: Where're you goin'?

Dragon: Under.

Sarah: What?

Dragon: Under.

Sarah: Under what?

Dragon: Underground dragon paths.

Silence. The Dragon has disappeared.

Lily:	Underground dragon paths! Come on, Sarah.

They rush to a large trunk. They open it and take out various items. The trunk has "Brother of Mr. Kwong, Feng Shui Advisor" written on it.

Lily:	Some people are guided by stars, and people who read the stars are astrologers, right?
Sarah:	Right.
Lily:	And others are guided by dragon paths! Uncle was an expert on dragon paths. That's what it's called, Feng Shui, F-E-N-G-S-H-U-I, like astrology, Sarah.
Sarah:	I don't know, Lily.
Lily:	We will find the path of the Dragon, and it will make everything clear.

Lily consults the book from the trunk.

We need help – you and you, come please.

They pass out cymbals, gong, drums to the children.

Lily:	Yes, you, and you, too. We need help. No noise and then beautiful noise. That's how it works.
Sarah:	What's this?

Red and orange banners.

Lily:	The colours of joy. J-O-Y! We've got to raise them high. It's going to work, Sarah. I know it!
Sarah:	I can't hold this all by myself.
Lily:	Get help! We need it to help us find the dragon paths.

The red and orange banners are mounted on something like a maypole. The pole has a Dragon head on top. The pole is held by Sarah or one taller audience member, and the banners are held up by others like awnings. Sarah solicits help.

Lily:	And on bright yellow scrolls the image of dragon. Hold it up. And now...C-O-M-P-A-S-S.

She removes a great wooden compass-like construction.

Mr. Kwong:	Lily!
Mr. Lowe:	What are you two doing?

Mr. Kwong:	You've broken into Uncle's Feng Shui trunk!
Mr. Kwong:	Put down the compass.
Mr. Lowe:	What's all this paraphernalia?
Lily:	P-A-R-A-P-H-E…

As she's getting things out.

Mr. Kwong:	No more spelling!

Takes the dictionary.

Lily:	But I have an idea, Father.
Mr. Kwong:	I don't want to hear it.
Lily:	Dragon paths, Father.
Mr. Lowe:	There's no dragons here.
Lily:	We're here, aren't we? And if Chinese Canadians are here, why not Chinese Dragons?
Mr. Lowe:	I'm sure there's a rule somewhere.
Lily:	They are here. Prairie Dragons. And maybe we can find the reason for the drought and the barn falling down and everything, if we can just find and read the Dragon paths. It can't be because Sarah and I are going against nature.
Sarah:	'Cause we aren't!
Mr. Kwong:	This may be something to think about.
Lily:	To do, not to think.
Mr. Kwong:	Uncle isn't here. Who would work the compass?
Lily:	You, Father. Couldn't we try?
Mr. Kwong:	I will try.

He takes the compass.

Lily:	This way everyone.
Lily:	Scrolls up!
Sarah:	Banners high.
Lily:	Are the instruments ready?
Mr. Lowe:	Ridiculous!
Mr. Kwong:	We need Dragon Dancers, nothing can be done without Dragon Dancers.

Lily:	A dragon must dance for Feng Shui.
Mr. Lowe:	Don't look at me.
Lily:	*(to audience)* Help.

> *A small cloth version of the original Dragon on sticks is manipulated by members of the audience.*

Mr. Kwong:	In order, all. Standing here, here and here.
Lily:	Be careful. The hole for the foundation is there.
Sarah:	Right there.
Lily:	Don't fall in.
Mr. Kwong:	*(picks up the big wooden compass)* I believe we're ready.
Lily:	Now!

> *The Stage Manager switches on sound/music; the cymbals, gongs, drum and bells ring, the little Dragon dances on its sticks, but Mr. Kwong is whipped around the playing area as if his hands are glued to the compass and the compass has gone mad trying to shake him off.*

Mr. Lowe:	That's enough!...Stop!...Stop! You're a grown man, Mr. Kwong!

> *Eventually, Mr. Lowe runs to help Mr. Kwong. He grabs the compass from him.*

Mr. Lowe:	Told you it was ridiculous. Dragons. Wooden compasses to find dragon paths. I never heard of anything so –

> *The compass goes mad yanking Mr. Lowe about the stage, eventually throwing him like a bucking bronc.*

Mr. Kwong:	Are you all right, Mr. Lowe?
Mr. Lowe:	Ohhhhh.
Mr. Kwong:	Not a good idea, Lily.
Mr. Lowe:	A bad idea.
Mr. Kwong:	You make my heart heavy, Lily. Let's go home. Everybody go home. Leave the things and go. I apologize for my stupid daughter. Everybody home. Come, Mr. Lowe, let me assist you.
Lily:	I'm sorry. It was a stupid idea.
Sarah:	But worth a try, Lily.
Lily:	I'm sorry, no, I don't think so.

Lily picks up the wooden compass.

Lily: It feels light. It feels…powerful and light. It sings, Sarah. I hear it singing.

Her hands holding the compass extend forward.

It's moving…leading me forward…

Mr. Lowe: Look!

Mr. Kwong: Yes.

Lily: *(music as Lily is led by the compass in a gentle, dipping dance that maps out a dragon path ending near the foundation site)*

This is the path of a dragon
tunneling   twisting and turning
sinuous mazy meander
a coil and a writhe and a wind and
a dance in the dark of an
underground path of a dragon
tunneling   twisting and turning
sinuous mazy meander. Oh!

Lily stops at the edge of the foundation site.

Sarah: What is it?

Lily: Sarah, I know what's wrong, Sarah! Your Papa dug the foundation right into a dragon pathway. Quick, move the boards, move everything out of the way. That's it. That's it.

Sound of thunder.

Sarah: To the east…

Thunder.

to the west…

Thunder.

right overhead.

Lily: *(holds out her hand, palm up)* I think…

Sarah holds out her hand.

I think –

Sarah: I think rain, Lily!

Lily: The Dragon has smiled on us, Sarah! It's a new world, Father.

Mr. Lowe: It's raining.

Lily:	Things do change.
Mr. Kwong:	*(passes dictionary back to Lily)* Yes, Lily.
Lily:	Things are changing!
Mr. Lowe:	Rain!

> *Mr. Lowe and Mr. Kwong hurry away.*
>
> *Crack of lightning.*
>
> *A look passes over Lily's face.*

Lily:	Oh.

> *She starts to laugh. She puts her hand in her pocket and draws out the beautiful stone which is split in two pieces.*

I think...

> *She gives the stone to Sarah. Lily puts her hand in her pocket and cups a microscopic "something" in the palm of it as she withdraws it from the pocket.*

Look.

> *The two girls peer at what's in her hand.*

Sarah:	Teeny tiny –
Lily:	Head like a camel –
Sarah:	Ear like a cow –
Lily:	Neck like a snake –

> *The microscopic Dragon begins to float up, up, up to the sky, and their focus follows it up as they speak.*

Sarah:	Belly of frog –
Lily:	Scales of carp –
Sarah:	Teeny tiny eagle claws –
Lily:	Teeny tiny tiger paws –
Sarah:	And a tail –
Lily:	Tail –
Sarah:	Tail of a dragon.

Dragon:	Tale of a Dragon ending.
	            Tale of two
	who leapt through the Dragon's Gate
	            achieved success

	by being themselves true to themselves.
Voice Off:	*(snotty English accent)* Stridulate.
Lily:	S-T-R-I-D-U-L-A-T-E.
Voice Off:	Trachea.
Lily:	T-R-A-C-H-E-A.
Voice Off:	Xyster.
Lily:	X-Y-S-T-E-R.
Voice Off:	Yttrium.
Lily:	Y-T-T-R-I-U-M.
Voice Off:	Zymurgy.
Lily:	Z-Y-M-U-R-G-Y!
Sarah:	Hurray!
Dragon:	Speak to your Mama, Sarah.
Sarah:	*(by her Mama's gravestone)* The truth of the matter is this is the best farm in the whole district, Mama. Papa's gravestone will be goin' up next week, and the north wall for the new barn is built. I do still get scared.
	She touches the pearl necklace.
	But I got faith and hope and your pearl necklace. And…and Prairie Dragons!
Dragon:	Sail thro' the sky breathing clouds Burrow thro' earth leaving paths The end the end the end
	Dragon disappearing, its tail seen last.
	of the Dragon's Tail.

The End

people cut-outs

Prairie Dragons stage set-up - front view
have dragon body parts - head with rolling eyes, body loop, tail - all manipulable and all separate
with the parts shoved underneath the ground cloth. Body part manipulators could even crawl out
underneath the ground cloth for effect.

manipulators

pusher under cloth to make
dragon under the earth

Swimmers
CLEM MARTINI

Design Concept by Douglas McCullough and James Andrews

CLEM MARTINI was born and raised in Calgary, Alberta, where he continues to make his home. He is a graduate of the University of Calgary and the National Theatre School's Playwriting Program. A three-time winner of the Alberta Culture and Multiculturalism Playwriting Competition, he has written stage and radio plays and short fiction. Clem Martini has recently collaborated on a film project on schizophrenia, *Shattered Dreams*, aired on the CBC's "Man Alive" series.

Swimmers was first produced by Chinook Theatre, Edmonton, Alberta, during the 1984-85 season with the following cast:

Father	Brent Fidler
Mother, Wendy	Katherine Schlemmer
Lyle	David Silvertsen
Brenner	Steven Hilton

Directed by Brian Paisley
Costume and Set Design by Barb Devonshire
Lighting Design by Mel Geary
Original Musical Score by Jamie Philp

CHARACTERS

Lyle	A thirteen-year-old with a not-too-bad pitching arm, recently has discovered the sport of swimming.
Mother	Lyle's Mother.
Father	Lyle's Father.
Brenner	A teammate on the swim team.
Wendy	Eleven years old, skinny as a rail, tongue like a knife when she uses it, swims like a fish.

Note: Wendy and the Mother can be double cast if necessary.

Swimmers

SCENE ONE

Lights come up on Lyle who is doing push-ups. First an ordinary series of push-ups and then push-ups with hand claps.

Mother: *(offstage)* Lyle?

> *Pause. Lyle continues his push-ups.*

Lyle?

Lyle: Yeah?

Mother: When?

Lyle: Soon.

> *Pause. He begins doing one arm push-ups.*

Mother: How soon?

It's late.

Lyle, have some consideration for my grey hairs. Put yourself in my shoes. How would you feel if it was past ten o'clock, and it was you down here listening to the floor creak and me up there still doing push-ups.

> *Lyle stops, exhausted, and rests with his face to the floor.*

Lyle: Amazed.

Mother: I heard that.

Okay, to bed now, or I strap on the boxing gloves and come up and take a round out of you.

Lyle: *(standing)* Okay. You win.

> *To audience.*

May 8th, 1984. It began a couple of nights ago. I'd finished working out and just gone to bed.

> *Calling downstairs.*

Night then, Ma.

Mother: Good night.

> **Basic Approach**
> use key light source to establish environment
>
> don't do anything special for conversations with the audience
>
> cue
> preset house lights to 1/2 and fade to bedroom overhead with maybe some light coming through a window

Lyle:	Pleasant dreams.
Mother:	Same to you.
Lyle:	Have a great sleep.
	Pause.
Mother:	Where are those boxing gloves?
Lyle:	Night.

bedroom out
leave nightlight coming
through window

(to the audience) I turned off the lights, lay down…

A bed is created by four people holding a sheet. Lyle lies in it.

cross to water effect
flood stage with blue top
light and clear side light
from low angle
light must not hit stage floor

use effects projectors with
some bounce-off water trays
with blue/green fronts with
horizontal clear plastic strips
moved slowly in front of the
lights

sound important to aid light
effect

Water. Everywhere. Above me, blue sky. Sunny. But no land in sight. Calm, peaceful. The sound of waves. No wind. No land either. As far as I can see, no land anywhere. I swim. What else can I do? Nothing but water. Funny kind of a dream, a dream with no land. That's even funnier. Thinking about a dream in the middle of a dream. I didn't think you could do that kind of thing. Still no land anywhere. Don't know why I'm not waking up. Well, if I can think of a dream in a dream, maybe I can think of a way out of the dream.

Voice:	Lyle!
Lyle:	That. Did you hear that? Someone calling me. I thought I heard someone calling me.
Voice:	Lyle!
Lyle:	Then I woke up. And it was as if the dream had actually happened. I could remember everything. Crazy.

SCENE TWO

cross to locker room
two or three clear or warm
overhead lights
no bedroom overhead

Sounds of swim practice going on in a pool. Water splashing. Whistle blowing. Coach yelling, "Let's get moving. C'mon, move it. One more lap. Hey…Hey…"

Lyle is dressing after swim practice. Brenner

is half dressed and is in the midst of having a towel fight with someone just outside the locker room door. He snaps the towel. Someone snaps a towel at him.

Brenner: Hey! Grow up!

Grow up I'm telling you!

He shuts the door and holds it shut while someone tugs to open it on the other side..

I'm warning you, you'll never be closer to death than you are now.

Lyle casually picks up a towel, leans over and gives Brenner a crack. Brenner lets go of the door.

You...

The door flies open and the fight is on again. Brenner races outside and the fight carries on out there. Moments later he returns exhausted.

I'm dead.

He flops down on the bench beside Lyle.

I was compelled to teach him the lesson of his life. That's the trouble with this swim team, too many boys, not enough men. And you're next Kennedy, for that little shot, you're next.

Lyle: I'm so frightened.

Brenner: You should be. Oh, I'm dead. Man, you take a long time to dress, Kennedy. My sister takes less time, and she puts on and takes off about thirteen different outfits before she's finished.

Lyle: Man, you talk a lot, Brenner.

Brenner: Yeah, but I have a lot of interesting stuff to say.

Coach is yelling.

Listen to that. I would just once like to see him yell like that at that great, great Pallidan.

Lyle: I guess she doesn't have to be yelled at.

Brenner: No, she doesn't have to be yelled at, what she needs is a good biff, right to the forehead. Wake her up a little. She drives me up the wall, she thinks she's sooooooo much. What I want to know is, like, is she stupid or what? She's never got anything to say. Just the face. You know, "The face." Like a mashed in pop can. What do you think, Kennedy, she stupid or what?

Lyle:	Don't think so.
Brenner:	What do you hang around with her for?
Lyle:	I don't hang around with her. She lives close to my place. I walk with her.
Brenner:	Don't know why she comes here, she doesn't seem to like anyone. But you.
Lyle:	As if. Besides, you should be glad she comes out, she's the best thing on this team.
Brenner:	I could swim as well as her if I was that skinny, too. Christly razor blade with two legs. She likes you, eh?
Lyle:	What's your problem? As if. She's two years younger than me.
Brenner:	Don't know. Susan McMurphy and me could have a thing going, and I'm two years younger than her.
Lyle:	Susan McMurphy? Susan McMurphy doesn't know you're alive.
Brenner:	Yeah, that's true. But if she did, we could have a thing going. So, there's no stopping a kid like Pallidan having…

Suddenly the changing room door flies open at the back, and a wet towel comes sailing in and hits Brenner in the head. Brenner races out.

Brenner comes back in.

	Some people are like having a slug for a pet. You can beat 'em all you like, but you can't teach 'em a thing. Hurry up, Kennedy! People are going to think we're falling in love in here.
Lyle:	So get dressed already. I'm done.
Brenner:	You ever seen a physique like this, Kennedy? Man. I don't know what I'm doing on this swim team. Training. Remember that – training. Swimming is good for the body. Hey, getting ready for baseball this season?
Lyle:	Yup.
Brenner:	Good year coming up. You pitching, me on third, Sotter on first and the Goulds out in field. Tell me we won't be sharp.
Lyle:	Yeah.
Brenner:	"Yeah." Try not to run off at the mouth so much will you, it's hard to keep up. How's the arm?
Lyle:	Good.

Brenner:	Good?
Lyle:	Yeah.
Brenner:	Feels good?
Lyle:	Yeah.
Brenner:	Feels okay then?
Lyle:	Yeah, it feels good!
Brenner:	All right, city finals this year!
Lyle:	You ready to go, or do you want to stay here a few more weeks?
Brenner:	Let's move. You want to come shoot some pinball for a bit?
Lyle:	Naw, I got to go home.
Brenner:	Sure?
Lyle:	Naw.

Coach is yelling.

Brenner: Listen to that sucker. If he yelled only once, just once at Pallidan, I think I would fall down dead with surprise.

They exit the locker room, and as they exit we hear a Beatle's tune.

Oh, oh. What have we here? It is Miss Perfection herself.

Enter Wendy playing the tune on her ghetto blaster. Ear phones are strung around her neck.

Are you ever skinny, Pallidan, you know that? That's not really a swimsuit you wear is it? Looks more like a straw with arm and leg holes cut in it.

Wendy stares at Brenner.

There it is. "The face."

Wendy: Oh. You're going to talk to me.

She puts the earphones on, plugs them into the machine and turns it up full blast.

Right. Talk.

Brenner:	You going with her, Kennedy?
Lyle:	She walks the same direction I do.
Brenner:	What you see in her I don't know.

He starts to exit. Wendy slips the earphones off.

Wendy: Hey Brenner! You call yourself an athlete? My dog swims better than you do. Beside you, my rubber duck looks like Olympic material.

Brenner: I bet you got one, too. You better take the little girl home. Must be time for her nap. Oh, yeah, and Pallidan, why don't you join the eighties and get some new music? The Beatles are dead you know. See ya, Kennedy.

Lyle: Bye.

Brenner exits.

Lyle: Hm.

Wendy: Ready to go?

cross to an alley of light, a roadway,
use leaf patterns for an exterior feel   *They start walking.*

Lyle: You know. You could try being a bit…nicer to him and the rest.

Wendy: Suppose.

Lyle: I mean. You'd have more friends if you were just…you know. Friendlier to people.

Pause.

Wendy: I'm glad you're walking me home.

Lyle: Why?

Wendy: Jane McVie said she was going to punch my face in.

Lyle: See. It'd pay to have a couple more friends.

Wendy: Who cares?

Lyle: Doesn't hurt to be friendly.

Wendy gives him a look.

Oh. "The Face."

Wendy: Your swimming's coming along.

Lyle: You think so?

Wendy: Get your kick down. Your kick is sloppy.

Lyle: Yeah.

Wendy: But. I was looking at you today, and you were looking okay. Coach noticed, too. You've really come along. Man! You used

	to be useless!
Lyle:	Yeah?
Wendy:	Yeah.
Lyle:	But, I have fun, eh? I don't know why exactly I took the dumb stuff in the first place, but I like it, you know? A lot.
Wendy:	Me, too. I love it. Two things I love. The Beatles and swimming. The trophies and all the rest of that...nothing. But swimming! It's, like, flying or gliding or I don't know. Something. Nothing like it. And then the Beatles.

She turns the Beatles up loud and starts dancing.

| Lyle: | Jesus. Cut it out. Look. Someone's going to see. |
| Wendy: | Who cares, who cares, who cares. |

Turns the music off.

We've passed the turnoff to McVie's place, so I guess she isn't going to punch my face in. Grab my heels. I want to try walking on my hands.

She flips over and Lyle grabs her heels.

| Lyle: | How can you get into so many fights? Hey, grow up! I don't want to do this. Feel stupid. |

Pause.

I'm going to let go.

Wendy:	I'll fall!
Lyle:	See, now you're acting stupid. Why do you do this kind of stuff?
Wendy:	Why do you hang around with me?
Lyle:	I don't hang around with you. I just walk home with you.
Wendy:	You could walk another way.
Lyle:	Are you coming up or what?

Wendy stops walking on her hands and looks up at Lyle.

| Wendy: | You're not a very good swimmer, Lyle. But I think you like swimming. And I like you. Let me down. You should hang around with me more often, you know. I think we could get to be friends. |
| Lyle: | You should get some friends your own age. |

Wendy:	Who cares about age? Everyone in my grade is a jerk. Everyone in your grade is a jerk but you. You like me, don't you?
Lyle:	Not everyone's a jerk, you know.
Wendy:	Yeah?
Lyle:	Yeah. And you know, you could probably get some friends your own age, if you wanted…
Wendy:	Get out. I got to go, I'm safe to walk home from here. Thanks. See ya later.
Lyle:	Bye.

SCENE THREE

cross to house interior: late afternoon light through window, light fixture over table - plan for both to vary interior scenes

Lyle enters his home. His parents are seated at the dinner table, eating.

Lyle:	Hi.
Mother:	Hello.
Father:	Hello.
Mother:	Supper's been prepared. It's warming on the stove.
Lyle:	Sorry I'm late.
Mother:	What happened?
Lyle:	Swimming practice went a bit long. Then I guess I got talking.
Father:	Wait. This is the third time this has happened in the past two weeks. And we had that talk about being late a couple of weeks before that. What do you think about that?
Lyle:	I don't know.
Father:	You know what time you're supposed to be here.
Lyle:	Yeah.
Father:	This isn't like you. Last reporting period some of your teachers said you don't seem to be paying attention. Are you feeling all right?
Lyle:	Yeah.
Father:	Is everything all right at school?
Lyle:	Sure. I'm just. I don't know. I won't be late again. I really am sorry.
	Pause.
Father:	You know what my Father would have done if you'd been late

for supper in his house?

Lyle: Whip you with a length of thick steel chain. Chop your ears off and pickle them. Drop you in a tub of smoking acid without blinking an eye. That sort of thing.

Long pause.

Father: That's right. Now go get your supper and let's not have this happen again.

Mother: Ah! Wash your hands first. Wash them, I said.

Lyle and she mock box.

Cut it out. Do something with him.

Father: Woman's work.

Mother: What's a man's work?

Father: Eating. Lyle, hurry up or I'll have your supper.

Lyle washes his hands, gets his supper.

Lyle: What is this?

Mother: Your Father made supper today.

Father: Potato pancakes.

Lyle: For supper?

Father: Why not?

Lyle: No reason, I guess.

Father: This was the sort of thing I was raised on, and it never hurt me any. So, who were you talking to that kept you so late?

Lyle: You know. The team. Brenner. Wendy.

Father: You walk her home again?

Lyle: Kinda.

Father: Huh. How's she doing at school now?

Lyle: Don't know. Not so well, I guess.

Father: Not breaking windows anymore?

Lyle: That was two years ago.

Father: Ohhh.

Pause.

Mother: What do you talk about with her?

Lyle:	Nothing much.
Mother:	What? Swimming?
Lyle:	Yeah.
Mother:	School?
Lyle:	Yeah, a little.

Pause.

Mother: I don't know, Lyle. I wish you wouldn't hang around with her so much. She's two years younger than you. She runs around wild. She's got no friends. You've got nothing in common with her. It looks funny.

Father: What ever happened to Brenner? He used to come here all the time.

Lyle: Nothing's happened. I still see him.

Father: Liked that fellow. Nice boy. Good third baseman, too. Good arm. He's coming out for the ball team again this summer, isn't he?

Lyle: Think so.

Father: And he's on this swim team, too?

Lyle: Yeah.

Father: Hm. Doesn't she have any, you know, girl friends her own age?

Lyle: Don't know, Dad.

Father: Why you? Why does she hang around with you?

Mother screams.

Father: Lord! What!

Mother: Get out! Get out!

She runs to the window and throws something.

Lyle: *(to the audience)* Here we go.

Father: What the hell is going on?

Lyle: *(to the audience)* Cats.

Mother: Cats! That big tabby is digging up the garden. Get out! You...

Lyle: *(to the audience)* They're only cats.

Father: They're only cats.

Mother: Well, they give me the creeps.

Lyle:	*(to the audience)* When I was five…
Mother:	When I was five I can recall my Mother finding a big black Siamese cat sitting in the crib on my baby brother's face, nearly smothering him. Licking its lips. Blinking. It still gives me the shivers.
Father:	Well, it gives me more than the shivers to hear you scream like that. My heart almost went. Give me a warning next time, raise a flag or something.
Mother:	*(sitting)* How'm I supposed to warn you, I never know when they're going…
Father:	There's one now!
Mother:	*(leaping up)* Where?

Father roars with laughter.

Mother:	You are so funny.
Father:	There.

Choking with laughter.

Licking its lips. Blinking.

Mother:	Are you through? You are not a well man. Finish your supper.
Lyle:	Aren't you having any?
Mother:	I finished before you came home. Those are all for you.

Pause.

Lyle:	Do cats eat potato pancakes?
Mother:	Not hungry?
Lyle:	Not so much.
Father:	*(takes them)* More for me. They'd have tasted better if you would have had them while they were still hot. You can't expect to just come in whenever and eat.
Lyle:	I know.
Father:	Maybe that's the way they do it over at the Pallidan's, but it's not the way we do it here. I don't know. I just don't know. Sure wish I could figure what it was you see in her.
Lyle:	I don't see anything. I'm just…walking.
Father:	You've been coming home an hour and a half, two hours late. Where do you walk to? She only lives three blocks up.

Pause.

What do you do?

Pause.

Well?

Lyle: I already said. We talk.

Father: Do you feel sorry for her, is that it? I mean you used to hang around with a pretty athletic crowd.

Lyle: Geez, SHE IS athletic. She's a better swimmer than me, she's a better swimmer than Brenner. She's the best swimmer in the city probably, maybe in the province, for her age. She's probably the most "athletic" person I know, so what's the problem? What am I...

He trails off.

Mother: That's no way to speak to your Father, Lyle.

Father: If you can't speak civilly after gallivanting about with her, you can hardly be surprised if we don't think highly of her.

Pause.

Well. If you don't want to talk, then maybe you should just go up to your room.

Lyle: Good.

Mother: Lyle.

Father: Fine. That's what you want?

Lyle: Sure. Why not?

Father: Okay then.

Lyle: Okay.

Stands.

Father: And if you feel like talking with us later, then you can come down and apologize.

Pause.

Lyle: I'll just go up to my room then.

Lyle exits.

Father: Don't know what's going on with him.

Lyle: So what if people think she's weird. Did you ever think some people think you're weird?

Mother: That's enough.

Father: No allowance for a month!

Lyle: *(to the audience)* You ever notice that it's those last shots that feel the best that end up hurting the most?

> *Slams the door behind him.*

You ever notice how when you slam a door, you feel good for a second, and then you feel stupid?

> *Pause.*

You ever notice how you think of the best things to say *after* you slammed the door?

> *Pause.*

You ever notice how dull a room is when you're sent up to it? So anyway, I didn't feel like reading a book, and I didn't feel like building a model, and I didn't feel like drawing. I had some homework to do, but I sure didn't feel like doing that.

> *Pause.*

What I really felt like doing was going out there and telling them off, but I didn't feel like getting grounded for a month, too. So I lay down on the bed. And I took a nap. It felt good to rest. Just lie back and relax and forget everything. Everything. Forget everything.

> *Everything is transformed, and Lyle is brought back into the Swim World.*

shift to water effects
add shafts of sunlight and
perhaps a warmer top light

Suddenly...

> *He blows water out of his mouth. Shakes his head.*

I was back...in that place. Again, nothing but water. Everywhere. The sun shining down. It was just setting a few minutes ago. This is very weird. A very weird dream. Okay, I'm going to wake up.

> *He pinches himself.*

I can't. Well, let's see. No land anywhere, so I guess. I'll swim...that way.

> *He swims.*

Hey, this is all right. This is...kind of fun. I can't believe how fast I'm swimming. This is great! Yo! And then suddenly I saw something. Ahead of me. Coming towards me. Fast. The waves kept slapping me in the face. I couldn't see...exactly what it was. So I decided to take off. But whatever it was that was following me, it was faster than I was. I couldn't out swim it. So I turned around...to meet it. Fight if I had to.

Wendy: Lyle!

Lyle: Wendy? Wendy! What are you doing here?

Wendy: *(smiles and treads water, looks about herself)* I made the place. What do you think? Something, eh?

          She dives.

Lyle: What do you...

          She comes back up.

          You made the place?

Wendy: Sure. C'mon.

          The two of them take off, swimming together. Racing, diving, swimming beneath and above the water, having a great time. Finally, they slow down.

          Isn't it great?! I knew you'd like it.

Lyle: What do you mean, you made the place?

Wendy: I dreamt it.

Lyle: You...

          He chokes as a wave hits him in the face.

Wendy: Oh, I forgot, you're new here. You want to float? Let's float.

Lyle: What do you mean, you made the place?

Wendy: I made this place in my dreams. It started off as just a lakey-kind of thing. You know, water. But I kind of pushed it out further and further. And invented things. I invented the waves. Great stuff, eh? Yeah, at first it was just flat, like a pool, but I thought, "Why not waves?" and there they were. And I made it bigger. And now it's started to do things on its own. There are fish here now, and I can't have had anything to do with them because I don't know anything about fish. And they are really great! All different colours, thousands of them in what-d-ya-call-em? Schools. Whoooosh! Just like a rainbow in front of you. Isn't it wonderful?

Lyle: Well. It's pretty weird.

Wendy:	Have you noticed that you don't get tired? That's another thing this place invented. You can swim for hours and not feel it at all. I know. I've done it. Aren't you excited? You're the only other person who knows anything about it.
Lyle:	Yeah. Thanks. It's...quite something. How'd you get me here anyway?
Wendy:	I called you, and you came. I'd been thinking about doing it for a while actually. I called you here a while ago, but you took off before I could get hold of you. I knew if I called again, you'd come back though. It's because you like swimming. You know? Like it. More than the contests and the competitions and all. You know?
Lyle:	Uh, yeah. But, uh, where's the beach?
Wendy:	There isn't any. As far as I know, anyway.
Lyle:	There isn't any?
Wendy:	Not as far as I know. I never thought any up. And I haven't seen any.
Lyle:	*(agitated)* No beach? Anywhere?
Wendy:	I don't even think there's a bottom to this, Lyle.
Lyle:	No bottom?

He chokes on more water.

Wendy:	I don't think so. I never seen any. I've tried diving, and you can dive an awful long way here, and there wasn't any that I could see. Just water, straight down. For miles, maybe hundreds of miles. I don't know. Maybe it's just water forever.
Lyle:	You're kidding?
Wendy:	Don't worry, Lyle. You can go back whenever you want. Just try to enjoy...
Lyle:	There's got to be some land somewhere...
Wendy:	Just relax...

Lyle starts choking again.

Lyle! Just relax...Lyle...

Lyle is back in his bedroom. Thrashing about. On his bed.

Lyle:	No! Ah, no.

He wakes up.

Ah!

He breathes deeply.

cross back to bedroom (*to the audience*) And I was back. In my bedroom. Ah. Oh. Back in my bedroom. Whew.

He pats the bed.

Mother: Are you all right?

She opens the door.

Mother: Are you all right?

Lyle: Yeah. Yeah, thanks.

Mother: You were…yelling.

Lyle: I know. I had a bad dream.

Mother: You're all right now?

Lyle: Sure. Yeah.

Mother: Good.

Pause.

Okay.

Pause. She starts to go.

Lyle? I didn't mean to yell at you downstairs.

Lyle: Oh. No, I'm sorry. I mean, me neither. I didn't mean it.

Mother: I knew you didn't. Good night, then.

Lyle: Night.

Mother: No more bad dreams.

Exiting.

That yelling scared me half to death.

Lyle lies back down.

Lyle: (*to the audience*) I couldn't wait until tomorrow. I had a lot of questions I wanted to ask Wendy.

SCENE FOUR

Sound of a school buzzer. Then sound of people in the halls, running as they leave for home.

Lyle: Wendy! Hey!

Lyle whistles through his teeth.

Hey!

He takes off her earphones.

Earth calling Wendy. Come in, Wendy.

cross to hallway
corridor of light – perhaps
the road, but bluish as if
under florescent lights
make stage look somewhat
washed out

Wendy: Yeah?

            Pause.

Lyle: How ya doin'?

Wendy: All right. Yourself?

Lyle: Good. Um.

(to the audience) It suddenly occurred to me that maybe it had been…just a dream. I mean, what was I going to say, "Were you, by any chance, dreaming the same thing the same time I was last night?" That's the kind of thing they lock you away for.

Wendy: Yeah?

Lyle: Ah…so. How was your day?

Wendy: Lousy. You?

Lyle: Lousy? How come lousy?

Wendy: I flunked out in English.

Lyle: How bad?

Wendy: Bottom of the class.

Lyle: That bad.

Wendy: Fershwiler handed them out in order of mark. I was last. She said it was a disgrace.

Lyle: To you?

Wendy: To the whole class.

Lyle: What'd you do?

Wendy: Ripped it up.

Lyle: Oh.

Wendy: Who cares about any stinking test? You know?

Lyle: What happened then?

Wendy: She kicked me out of class. I need a note from my Mother to get back in.

Lyle:	You study?
Wendy:	I thought I did.
Lyle:	What are you going to do?
Wendy:	Get a note, I guess.

Pause.

My Mother won't give me a note. She won't do it.

Lyle:	Why not?
Wendy:	Who knows? She just won't, that's all. Doesn't believe in it or something. Who cares? Who cares? Everybody laughed. Everybody. She said somebody in grade three could have done better.
Lyle:	I flunked out of English last term. It's not too crisp all right.
Wendy:	Yeah, but you only did it to show off that you could flunk as well as anyone. I just want to pass a course. Any course.

Pause. Wendy continues to just stand there.

Lyle:	It's no big deal.
Wendy:	I know. Who says it's any big deal? It's no big deal. But. I just wanted to pass, that's all. I'm not going to make it this year. I can feel it. I can feel it. It's not just this class. It's everything. Every class.
Lyle:	Don't worry. There's still, you know, time. And let's say you stay behind another year. That's not such a big deal either.
Wendy:	Oh, Jesus.

She laughs.

Oh, Jesus. Maybe it's not a big deal for you.

She begins to break down.

But Lyle. Another year? Of this? Tests and laughing and everything all the time. Oh, God. I'm such a retard.

Lyle hustles her out of the middle of the hallway.

Lyle:	Shh. Shh. Come here. Look, I can give you a hand, or something. Maybe I've got notes somewhere. It won't be that bad. You're not a retard. You're not. You've got something. Something. It's like, you are, you know,

Searching.

	just fine.
	Pause.
Wendy:	"Just fine?"
Lyle:	Yeah. Just fine. Is that dumb?
	Wendy starts to laugh.
	Yeah, I guess it is.
Wendy:	I am "just fine."
Lyle:	Well.
Wendy:	If anyone asks me how I am…
	Both finish the sentence together.
	I can tell them I am "just fine."
Lyle:	…You can tell them you are "just fine."
	Wendy continues laughing.
Lyle:	Boy, I really know how to help out, eh? Okay. Okay. So I guess I'm the retard.
Wendy:	No. No, you're just fine, too, Lyle. So. What did you think of "the place" last night?
	Long pause. Wendy laughs.
	It really knocked you over, didn't it?
Lyle:	Then…
Wendy:	Well? How'd you like it?
Lyle:	Just fine, I mean it was…great. Weird, but…how did you do that?
Wendy:	I just called and…
Lyle:	What do you mean you "just called"…
Wendy:	You showed up, it's hard to explain, but isn't it great? I mean…
Lyle:	Why didn't you warn me or any thing? One moment, I'm lying in bed…
Wendy:	I thought it would be a surprise, I didn't know you would be scared. You were scared weren't…
Lyle:	Course I was scared, I mean, think about it…
	Enter Brenner.

Brenner:	Hi, Kennedy. Hi, Wonder Woman. You know, I was talking with my little brother, and he tells me you flunked out in English today.
	Wendy looks up. Looks to the side. Looks down.
Wendy:	I got to go. See ya.
Brenner:	What a freak.
Wendy:	*(Wendy stops)* You know. You know, you say that all the time. And you know, you are such a total jerk.
Brenner:	Why don't you just admit that you're an ugly little girl who can't do anything but swim. It's no wonder you're always in the water, 'cause there's no one who likes you on dry land.
	Wendy nods. Looks down and then punches him hard.
Lyle:	Oh, geez, c'mon, Brenner. Wendy.
Brenner:	You know, if you were a boy, I'd kick your head in.
Wendy:	If I were a boy you wouldn't be able to.
	Brenner pushes Wendy hard. Lyle grabs him by the shoulder.
Lyle:	Look, Jim. She's just a kid…
	Brenner wheels around and hits Lyle.
Brenner:	There. You're always running around on her shirttails. How do you like that?
Lyle:	What are you doing?
Brenner:	Come on. Come on.
	Pushes Lyle.
Wendy:	Leave him alone.
Lyle:	I don't want to do this.
	Brenner pushes him, and then pushes him again.
	I don't want to do this.
Brenner:	Come on.
	Pushes him.
	Come on!
	Lyle pushes him back. Immediately he regrets it and turns to the audience with his hands up in a "Time out" signal.
Lyle:	*(to the lighting operator)* Time out. Could we just skip on past this

scene?

Looks at Brenner.

It's not going to be a pretty sight.

SCENE FIVE

Lights snap to black. Count of a few   cross to roadway - cooler
seconds, and they snap back up with Lyle   feel
and Wendy walking along, Lyle holding a
kleenex to his nose and mouth.

Wendy: I'm sorry.

Pause.

Are you okay?

Reaches for the kleenex.

Lyle: Don't.

Wendy: What did I do?

Pause.

You're not going to talk to me now, is that it?

Pause.

You've got some nerve, you know. What did I do? I didn't do anything. So you got beat up, who asked you to? You think I haven't been beaten up? I've been beaten up.

Lyle: That's not it.

Wendy: Then what is it?

Lyle: You don't know, do you? You don't have to watch what you do, you don't have to watch what you say. No, no, not you. You're above all that kind of stuff. You just say what you like and whatever happens, happens. You didn't have to ask me! What was I going to do? Let you get beat up? So do what you want, be above it all. But do it when I'm not around, 'cause I like having a few friends, and I don't like having my face punched in.

Wendy: You're just like all the rest.

Lyle: Who said I wasn't? Jesus, I am all the rest! People like me, or they did.

Pause.

Wendy: Not me. Not anymore.

Exit Wendy.

Lyle: Yeah, yeah.

Pause.

(to the audience) I am so stupid. I get into a fight with Brenner over Pallidan and then get into a fight with Pallidan. Everybody ends up hating me. It seemed from that moment on, everything came at me faster and faster.

A couple of people rush past Lyle, walking backwards quickly, as though Lyle were walking extremely quickly. A dog races past at superhuman, or rather superdog speed, and utters a couple of high-pitched, ultrasonic squeaks.

I just couldn't seem to catch my breath. I went home, and Mom made a big fuss...

Mother: Lyle!

cross to interior of house

Lyle: About the bleeding nose. There's something about bleeding noses that brings out the "ahhhh" in mothers. And I got a lecture from her about fighting, and I thought that would be an end to it, but when things get going they really get going.

SCENE SIX

Enter Father.

shift the quality of the interior light - perhaps darker with more sense of light from the fixture over the table

Father: Hi.

Lyle: I was going out for a walk later that evening.

(to Father) Hi.

Father: Where you off to?

Lyle: Don't know. Nowhere. For a walk.

Father: Oh. Brought something for you.

Lyle: Oh, yeah?

Father: Yeah. Catch.

Throws him some swimming goggles.

I remembered you saying something about

	the water and your eyes. Chlorine in 'em.
Lyle:	Yeah. That was a couple of months ago, I've got some since then. But thanks anyway. They're nice.
Father:	Well. You can keep them as spares.
	Pause.
Lyle:	Sure.
	Tries them on.
	They fit. Great.
Father:	Good.
Lyle:	Yeah. Thanks.
Father:	You got a moment, or am I keeping you from a real pressing walk.
Lyle:	No.
Father:	So you think we might talk?
	Pause.
Lyle:	About what?
	Pause.
Father:	What do you think of my job?
Lyle:	Don't know. I guess it's a good job.
Father:	Bull. It's a job for a pea brain.
Lyle:	If you say so.
Father:	I know so. I got a pea brain, so it's a good job for me. Decent pay, good union. You. What do you think is the most important thing about school?
Lyle:	Don't know.
Father:	Is there anything you do know?
Lyle:	Don't know.
	Pause.
	Grades, I guess.
Father:	Bull. Grades are the least important thing.
Lyle:	That's not what you said when I got that F in English.
Father:	That was something else, but the most important thing about

school is how you get along with people. You make the right connections in school, learn how to get along with the right people, when you graduate you'll do all right. You make the wrong connections and later on you won't stand a chance.

Pause.

You understand any of this?

Lyle: I guess so.

Father: I didn't think so.

Lyle: Why ask me then?

Pause.

Father: You won't like it, but someday you're going to find out that there are some things that I knew more than you because I was older. You learn from experience. I know this about me, I'm just another stupid labourer. I know how I got to be this way, first of all

Points to his head.

not enough here. But there were others, same as me, who went on to make good, and they knew the right people. Knew how to behave.

You don't have to worry about this.

Taps his head.

Nothing wrong with you there. Besides that F in English. You're a bright kid, not like me. That's fine. You do good in school and sports. Again, fine. But hang around with trouble-makers, and you get trouble. I can't let you do that. If it means doing some things now that you don't like, that's my job as a father. I don't want you hanging about with this little what's-her-name, Wendy, anymore. I don't know what you see in her, and at this point, I don't care.

Lyle: She's on the swim team, how am I supposed to not see her?

Father: Swim with her, train with her, but I don't want to hear about you walking her anywhere or hanging about after school with her.

Pause.

Lyle: You can't stop me.

Father: I can. If I find out that you are, I'll keep you home. No swimming. No baseball. No football.

Lyle:	It's not fair.
Father:	That's the way it is. It's for your own good.
Lyle:	How'm I supposed to argue with "It's for your own good." I know what's for my own good.
Father:	Sure. You hang around with some girl two years younger than yourself, get into fights with her. She's the wrong people for you.
Lyle:	How do you know who's the wrong people for me?
Father:	Okay. So, that's that. If you're going to go for a walk, you better be back in an hour.

He exits.

> slowly shift light to a neutral quality, perhaps based on the bedroom but not too specific

Lyle: *(to the audience)* I do all the yelling and win none of the arguments.

> don't try to keep up with each location

Pause.

I argue with Dad over whether or not I'll see Wendy, and she's already told me that she doesn't want to see me any more. I sure don't get any smarter. Everything kept getting quicker and quicker and quicker. I'd barely gone to bed…

He takes off his shirt.

when it was time to go to school again.

Alarm rings and he puts his shirt back on and exists.

And school wasn't any better the next day.

At school. The bell rings and Lyle picks up some books and opens them. Another bell rings and he closes them.

> return to halfway of scene four

I was glad when it was over, but of course I had to run into Wendy over by the lockers.

SCENE SEVEN

He walks past Wendy. She stares at him the whole way.

Lyle:	What are you staring at?
Wendy:	Nothing.

She turns away.

Lyle:	Look.
Wendy:	Don't bother talking to me.

Enter Brenner, dribbling a basketball down the hallway.

Brenner: Thumpa, thumpa, thumpa. Here he is, Abdul Karim Brennar making his way down the court. He pivots...Hello.

Wendy simply turns away and ignores him.

Hey, Pallidan. 'Bout that athletically inclined dog of yours that can swim better than me. This town isn't big enough for the two of us. Tell it to grab its shorts and sneaks and meet me in the main gym at High Noon tomorrow, and if it can play basketball better than me too, I'll not only quit beaking off, but I'll be on the very next train out of town.

Wendy turns to go. Brenner snags her.

Whoops. And he snags her on the rebound.

Brenner picks Wendy up.

Lyle: Brenner...

Wendy: Mind your own business. Put me down.

Brenner: Certainly.

He drops her, or rather stuffs her in a garbage barrel in such a fashion that she is immobilized.

Dunk shot!

Wendy: Pick me up.

Brenner: There's no pleasing some people. Well, gotta go. Got hands to shake, autographs to sign. See you in the funny papers.

He picks up his ball.

You gave me a sore jaw, Kennedy. Nothing like what you got, but not bad.

He exits. Wendy is struggling to get out of the garbage can. Lyle goes over to help.

Wendy: I don't want...I don't need your help! Get away from me!

She breathes deeply and closes her eyes. Stands perfectly still.

Lyle: Are you all right? What are you doing?

Wendy: I'm thinking about what it would be like if I could destroy the whole world. Everything.

Lyle: Great thought.

Wendy: You think I'm kidding. I'm not. I hate it here. I just hate it.

Totally miserable suddenly.

Just leave me alone, will you.

Lyle: *(to the audience)* She wasn't at swim practice on the weekend, and she didn't make it to school on Monday. Nobody missed her. Nobody even noticed, I think, except maybe the swim coach. I walked home alone, like I did before I met her. But things didn't seem to slow down any. Sometimes it seemed that people were even talking quicker.

SCENE EIGHT

cross to interior - perhaps a later-at-night feel with cool light through window, but maybe save this for Scene Nine if a change is desirable, otherwise no change

Telephone rings.

Lyle: Hello. Hm? I'm sorry, I can't understand what you're saying, could you please slow down. Oh. Hi. Wendy's Mother. She was upset. Yeah, Mrs. Pallidan. Yeah. Uh, no. I haven't seen her since Friday. I thought she was sick or something. She's missing? I was the last one to see her? Well, that was last week…and you haven't seen her since? Yeah. Yeah, we had an argument. But. But. I haven't seen her. What do you want me to do? I didn't do anything. I haven't had a thing to do with her running away or whatever. You want to speak to my Mother? What for? Look, Mrs. Pallidan… MOM!

Mother: What?

Lyle: Mrs. Pallidan wants to speak to you.

Mother: Who?

Lyle: Wendy's Mother.

Mother: What does she…

Lyle: Just talk with her, will you?

Mother: Hello? Yes. Yes? That's terrible. Have you phoned the police? I don't understand. I hardly think that my son would have anything to do with it. She seems perfectly capable of doing that sort of thing on her own without any coaching from Lyle. What do you mean Lyle has been a bad influence? If anything, it's the other way around…

Lyle: *(to the audience)* Parents!

Lyle rubs his forehead.

I didn't know what to do. I kept running through what I could do in my mind, but I didn't come up with any answers. After dinner I tried talking with Mom.

SCENE NINE

Lyle:	Ma?
Mother:	Yes?
Lyle:	Um. Do you think it's possible for someone to…escape into their dreams?
Mother:	No.

Pause.

Lyle:	Oh. Okay. Have you ever heard of anyone doing anything like that?
Mother:	No.

Pause.

Lyle:	Suppose, I said. That I knew. Someone…who…

Sighs.

Oh.

Pause.

Mother:	Is this what that bad dream you had the other night was about?
Lyle:	*(doubtfully)* Kinda.
Mother:	I told you you shouldn't be watching those movies. It's just that kind of thing that gives you nightmares.
	(to Lyle's Father) I told you that those late night science fictions weren't the thing for Lyle.
Father:	*(from off)* Let him watch whatever he likes. He can always ask us about them later, if there's anything he doesn't understand.
Mother:	Sure.
Father:	How else will he learn to handle things?
Mother:	From science fiction and horror movies he learns how to handle life. Ha!
Father:	From those and everything else.
Mother:	He's only a boy. When he's older, then he can watch what he wants. Be reasonable.
Father:	How will he learn to handle anything when he's older if you keep him from handling anything now? What are these nightmares about?

Long pause. Lyle gets up, flaps his arms three times, rolls his eyes, chirps like a monkey and barks three times. Quickly.

Lyle: That.

Lyle walks out.

Father: Hm.

Mother: I knew adolescence would be tough, but...

Father: Maybe it's the heat.

They exit.

Lyle: (*to the audience*) What did people want from me? Almost nobody knew her. Those that did didn't like her. Those that did like her couldn't find her. I was the only one that could find her, and I didn't know if I could get there, or what I would do once I did. Course, she'd gone to the Swim World. Where else? I couldn't tell Mrs. Pallidan that though. Or my parents. Or the cops. I went for a walk, tried to figure out what to do. Obviously, I had to do something. No one else could. Go and get her, I guess. But how? I tried just thinking about her and the Swim World, but that didn't get me anywhere. I tried calling her with my mind. It felt stupid, but I tried.

the feeling should be a field at night with moonlight, patterns of trees and leaves close by

shoud be dim but not dark with some background environmental sound

Pause.

Nothing. I figured I might as well try lying down, 'cause that's what I'd been doing every other time I went. Maybe it would relax me, or concentrate me, or something. And if you don't think it feels dumb lying down in a field, you should try it sometime. I lay there, and thought about her...the way I last saw her. And then. It was like a giant fist grabbed me, shook me and tossed me through the air. And when I should have hit the ground...there wasn't any ground to hit anymore. I was there. The Swim World.

Only this time it was different. Waves roared up and down everywhere, big ones that drove you under and made you come up

*Storm
needs sound
increase speed and violence of effects and add some top lights (four or five) in lavender and red that can pulse and move during the scene (this adds mystery and violence)*

gasping for air. Cold rain poured down, and a wind screamed along the top of the water tearing the foam off the waves and whipping it in your face. I tried to catch my breath, but couldn't. Every time I opened my mouth, the ocean rushed in. Staying up, up above the surface, took just about everything I had in me. For the first time I felt frightened for Wendy...Wendy! Wendyyyyyy! I went looking for her.

decrease violence of effects for the dialogue effects should vary throughout the scene

> *He swims.*

Wendy!

Wendy: Go away!

Lyle: *(to the audience)* She swam off. What could I do? I swam after her. Wendy! Wait up!

Wendy: No.

Lyle: She was the better swimmer, but maybe she wasn't concentrating, I don't know, but slowly...slowly, I began to catch up.

Wendy: Why don't you just get lost?

> *The two have been racing until now. Now, Wendy freezes in mid-stroke and Lyle stands.*

Lyle: Our coach on the swim team has always told us, "Listen up. You can fool me, you can fool your Mother, but you can't fool your body. Warm up! Always warm up before you race. Stretch your muscles. Get limber, or by crikey, you will be one sorry son of a gun someday."

> *The two start swimming in slow motion and gradually begin speeding up to a racing speed through the following talk. It should have the effect of a locomotive slowly building speed.*

I remembered this because...as I swam...trying to catch up with Wendy...swimming as fast as I could...as fast as I had ever swum...I tore a muscle. Ahhh!

> *Lyle stops and holds up his injured arm. Wendy swims back to see what has happened. Not too close, however.*

Wendy: What's the matter?

Lyle: I've pulled a muscle or something.

> *Pause.*

Wendy: Let me see. Float will you, float. Relax.

> *Pause.*

	I think you've ripped it. I suppose now you'll blame me for this too. I didn't ask you to come, you know.
Lyle:	I know.
Wendy:	Well, you'll have to go back.
Lyle:	How?
Wendy:	Do what you've done before.
Lyle:	I thought you sent me.
Wendy:	No, you did it. When you get scared, you blank all this out, and it sends you back. So just think about home, and blank out the Swim World.
Lyle:	Yeah, but you have to come, too.
Wendy:	Look, just leave me alone.
Lyle:	You can't stay here forever.
Wendy:	I can do whatever I want!
Lyle:	What about your parents? Your Mother called. She sounded worried.
Wendy:	Look! Will you shut up and take off!

She starts to leave. Lyle grabs with his good arm and tries to exit the Swim World.

Wendy:	Let go of me!

Lyle lets go.

Lyle:	It's not working.
Wendy:	What do you mean?
Lyle:	I tried. Nothing happened.
Wendy:	Try again. Think this time!
Lyle:	I must be doing something wrong.
Wendy:	You are so useless! Here! Give me your hand. Let me try.

Pause. Wendy is surprised.

I can't do it.

Pause. She tries again.

It's different. It's not letting us go.

Lyle:	What do you mean?

Wendy:	Usually, I just think. And it…I get home. But this time…
	She tries again.
	The place has changed. It's not letting us through.
Lyle:	Concentrate.
Wendy:	I can't.
Lyle:	Try.
Wendy:	I can't 'cause I'm upset, stupid, can't you see I'm upset? I can't think of anything to go back to because nothing seems good anymore. I can't concentrate. I can't get through. I can't do anything!
Lyle:	Well. Whatever. You do. You'd better do it. Quick. Because. I'm drowning, Wendy.
Wendy:	What?
Lyle:	I'm not kidding. I'm drowning.
Wendy:	Give me your hand!
Lyle:	*(to the audience)* And the giant's fist squeezed again. Ahhh! And then. I felt something soft and dry and prickly beneath my fingers…and I opened my eyes. And we were back home again. In the field behind my house. The ground was dry and dusty. The sky was clear and dark and filled with stars. No wind. No storm. Just crickets, frogs and a dog barking itself to sleep in an alley somewhere up the valley. Well. What happened?
Wendy:	I thought. How you were. My only…
	She turns away and mumbles.
Lyle:	What?
Wendy:	*(flatly)* I said I thought how I was losing the only friend I had. I guess it concentrated me. Because here we are. Of course, I was wrong, so. Excuse me.
Lyle:	Help me up.
	Wendy takes the wrong arm.
	Ow.
Wendy:	Sorry. You better get that looked at.
	She helps him up.
	What are you going to tell your parents about the arm?

(margin note) ross back to the field ⸱erhaps have it brighter ⸱nd more friendly

Lyle:	Tell them I threw it out while dreaming about "Three's Company." That ought to keep them going for a while.
Wendy:	What?
Lyle:	Nothing. What about you? What'll you tell your Mother?
Wendy:	Tell her I ran away.
Lyle:	Won't she want to know where?
Wendy:	Yeah. But if I don't tell her, what can she do?
Lyle:	She's going to be angry?
Wendy:	Yeah.

Pause.

Lyle:	You going to be okay?
Wendy:	Sure. Why not? Look. I guess I should be going.
Lyle:	Yeah. Uh.

Pause.

Thanks. I would have drowned. So. Thanks.

Wendy:	Well. You came out for me.

Pause

Thanks.

Pause.

Lyle:	It's okay.

Pause.

Oh, and Wendy...

Wendy:	Yeah?
Lyle:	Stick around this time. It's dull not having you to talk to. While you were gone I even went and bought my first Beatles cassette.
Wendy:	Which one?
Lyle:	"Abby Road."
Wendy:	Great, isn't it?
Lyle:	Yeah, it is. Meet me tomorrow at the end of the road, and we'll walk to school. I want to talk some more about this Swim World business. Okay?
Wendy:	Okay.

Lyle:	Okay. Night then.
Wendy:	Night.
Lyle: *cross to bedroom with* *overhead source on*	*(to the audience)* I went home, put a cold cloth on my shoulder. Figured if there was anything really wrong with it, I'd do something about it the next day.
Father:	*(from offstage)* Is that you?
Lyle:	Yeah.
Father:	Where've you been?
Lyle:	Out with the right kind of people.
Father:	What?
Lyle:	Just out in the yard.
Father:	What for?
Lyle:	Shooting stars, Dad. Lots and lots of shooting stars.
Father:	Oh.
Lyle: *overhead out with just* *light coming through the* *window*	*(to the audience)* And I went to bed. And I turned out the lights. And the bed didn't move, and I didn't go anywhere. *Lights start to fade.* But around midnight there was this rapping at my window. Who is it?
Wendy:	It's me. Here.
	She hands him a number of cassettes through the window.
Lyle:	What's this?
Wendy:	The Beatle's "White Album. The Best of the Beatle's, One" and "The Best of the Beatles, Two."
Lyle:	Thanks.
Wendy:	Got to go. Take care of them.
Lyle:	I will.
Wendy:	See you tomorrow.
Lyle:	Yeah. Tomorrow.
	Blackout.
cross to house and *post-show lighting*	***The End***

The lighting for this show is based on the concept that there should be no blackouts between scenes and that the various locations can for the most part be created by the lighting and the sound. Each locale should get a specific set of lights that suggests the particular type of space, such as the bedroom with an overhead light fixture and a window light that can be the source of night light when the overhead light is turned off. It is very important that there be some sounds associated with most of the spaces as such sounds do as much or more than the lights to create an environment. Such an approach would greatly reduce the need for scenery and time-consuming scene changes.

The problem of Lyle's dialogue directed to the audience should not get any particular or special treatment as it would become quite distracting to have the lights shifting back and forth as much as they would have to. Trust the actor in the existing light.

Side View

blue eye

bench type arrangement on casters

platform
weight

30" high

Detail

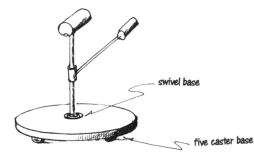

swivel base

five caster base

Friends

TOM BENTLEY-FISHER
with Patrica Grant

Design Concept by Tara Ryan

TOM BENTLEY-FISHER is an actor, musician, playwright and director who is currently Artistic Director at Twenty-Fifth Street Theatre Centre, Saskatoon, Saskatchewan. He has directed for theatres throughout Canada, including The Citadel, Theatre London, Theatre Direct, Adelaide Court and Arbor Theatre. From 1975-81 he was Director of the Professional Training Program in the Department of Drama at the University of Waterloo. Tom Bentley-Fisher's direction has twice been nominated for Dora Mavor Moore Awards for Most Outstanding Children's Theatre, and his production of *How I Wonder What You Are* received the 1984 Chalmers Award.

Friends was first produced by Theatre Direct Canada, Toronto, Ontario, and toured throughout Ontario elementary schools in the spring of 1984. The play was also a featured production at the Scarborough Fanfare Festival and the Toronto International Children's Festival with the following cast:

Todd	Blake Carter
Janice	Marina Endicott
Alex	Gary T. Furlong
Margaret	Barbara Barnes
Miss Dewson	Patricia Grant

Directed by Tom Bentley-Fisher and Patricia Grant
Designed by Roderick Mayne

PLAYWRIGHT'S NOTE

Friends is dedicated to Cherrywood Alternative School and Miranda. The Friends Project was developed from an idea by Jerome Ackhurst and Tom Bentley-Fisher. A first draft was workshopped by Barbara Barnes, Marina Endicott, Patricia Grant, Gary Furlong and Jerome Ackhurst. The creative input of these individuals into the final script is gratefully acknowledged.

the duck eggs are the central theme so they should be central to the action – ie, they should always be present

The play consists of a Prologue and 14 scenes taking place on 14 consecutive school days. Miss Dewson, supervisor of the daycare, has given the children a project – nine duck eggs to incubate and hatch. The timing of events in the play coincides with the latter half of the incubation period.

darker lghting
maybe some sort of dark-to -light changes can add to the calender and reality scenes

The daycare is located in a Public School open from early morning until 6 pm. The school age children are there before school, during lunch and after school. Some children arrive at 7 am. and are picked up at 6 pm. The day is very long. All the scenes take place during the latter part of the day.

use primary colours along with green, orange and purple

Although the location for the events is a particular corner of the daycare, the "free play area," the set itself is of a more abstract concept. It is a projection of a child's view of an "environment" created from cardboard boxes of all shapes and sizes. These boxes must be used as imaginatively by the actors as they would be by a group of children. Some boxes tower above them, some are small enough to sit on, crawl through, use as building blocks, etc. The children in the play have made rockets, drums, birds, hats and other costumes out of brightly painted boxes. The incubator is also represented by a cardboard box.

During the play some of the bigger boxes open to reveal large childlike paintings of birds, sunbursts, stars and flowers, and by the final scene the set has been transformed from "a pile of boxes" into a massive configuration of form and colour.

The days of the week and of the incubation period are marked at the beginning of each scene by some "calendar" device or chart, which "magically" flips over or reappears with the appropriate date and remains in place throughout each scene. This could also be a puppet-like placard, which rises in and out of one of the larger boxes.

The calendar progress is accompanied by a musical theme or rhythmic pattern, which should be flexible enough to reflect changes in mood and the gathering momentum of the plot.

CHARACTERS

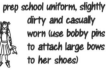

prep school uniform, slightly dirty and casually worn (use bobby pins to attach large bows to her shoes)

Margaret	A shy child recently enrolled in the Senior Kindergarten School Programme. She carries with her a small, furry toy elephant named Robert.

glasses, favourite baseball hat, loafers, the rest in wool, (looks like mom dressed him)

Todd	Grade One, an imaginative adventurer, who is still testing the limits of his independence.

skirt or sweat pants, trendy, updated clothes

Janice	Grade Two, a very organized little girl, who takes great pride in fulfilling the rules and regulations.

blue jeans, t-shirt, the tough look, untidy, sneakers

Alex	Grade Three, a "wheeler-dealer," who dominates the younger children with his superhero antics and streetwise skepticism.

youthful and relaxed dresser (escape from the horn-rimmed glasses image)

Miss Dewson	Supervisor of the Daycare, a teacher who cares for each child's individual needs and who believes in creating circumstances where children can solve problems through relating constructively to each other.

colours:
choose muted tones so as not to compete with the primary set

Friends

PROLOGUE

banging on boxes
drum beat starts out low
and slow, like a heartbeat
sound
this can then be
reincorporated later into the
                  ducklings hatching

knot rope

rocket box

From somewhere within the mass of cardboard boxes we hear drums. This quick series of introductory scenarios takes place in and amongst the boxes and catches Janice, Todd and Alex in various moments of play. The drumming continues to the end of the prologue.

Todd comes running in.

Todd: *(yelling to the top)* Lower the rope, Gert! Lower the rope and I'll save you. I'm not afraid of heights, Gert – lower the rope! Wait a minute – I'll go get my rocket – now hang on tight and don't slip till I get back.

Alex and Janice move through very fast in a two-headed box. Todd zooms across in his rocket. Alex starts drumming on a box like a rock star.

Alex: Just beat it - beat it - beat it - beat it - beat it - beat it - BEAT IT!

Janice enters wearing boxes on her feet.

Todd: We're best friends, Janice, right?

Janice: I'm testing for quicksands.

Todd: You wanna play wedding?

Janice: No, baby Todd.

Todd: You can be the bride this time.

Alex enters.

I'll be your best friend, Alex.

Alex: Okay, kid, okay – ya wanna play statue? – this'll be great Toddhead – okay, hold this –

Alex piles boxes on Todd.

this'll be great, now don't move till I get back.

He leaves.

What a weirdo!

Janice flies through in a bird box. Alex reenters and starts drumming again. Todd throws off the boxes.

Alex keeps drumsticks with him at all times

Todd: I'm not your friend, Alex.

Alex: You're a Toddhead, Toddhead.

Todd: I'll never be your best friend.

Alex: You're a Toddhead.

Janice enters and picks up a drum box.

Janice: You can be my best friend, Todd.

Todd picks up a drum box.

Todd: No.

Janice: Yes.

Todd: No.

Janice: Yes

Alex: No. No. No. No. No.

The three are playing "Yes, No" rhythms on their drums.

Todd: Yes. Yes. Yes. Yes. Yes.

Janice: Noooooooooooooooooooooooo.

Todd: Yes.

Alex: No.

Janice: Yes.

They dance around.

Janice, Todd & Alex:
        Yes. No. Yes. No. Yes. No. Yes. No...

The rhythm crescendos, ending in a loud:

(all three) Yeeeeeeeeeeeeeeeeeeeeeeeeeeeeeeeees!

They dance off as a large box moves to reveal Margaret alone on the stage. The drumming stops and the first chart "theme" is heard as the Duck Project Chart rises up to reveal "Tuesday, Day 12." This occurs at the beginning of each scene to mark the transition from day to day. It is important that the action of the play flows through these transitions and that each consecutive day "crossfades" into the next.

SCENE ONE

Margaret is standing by the duck egg box. Janice is enthusiastically "showing her the ropes." It is Margaret's first day in after-school care.

Janice: You don't have to be afraid, Margaret. It's very special. This is our project, Margaret – we get to have a project to do for 28 days. We have eggs – nine little eggs – Duck eggs! These little eggs will turn into ducks, Margaret. This is our PROJECT, Margaret, that we get to take care of. In this project, Margaret, everybody in the After Four Programme takes care of the eggs. We have to do things for them because there's no mother duck to take care of them. Everyday it's one person's duck-duty day, and you get to be responsible, to check the eggs, and look at this thermometer to see if it's at the right temperature, and sprinkle a little water on their shells so they don't get dry and crack. We have to be responsible. It takes 28 days, Margaret – and see, Margaret, see this, Margaret, this is our calendar – and it changes every day, and about DAY 28, or maybe DAY 27 or DAY 29 the ducks will be born. And sometimes, Margaret, I know it can be YOUR duty-day. You can be responsible. Don't worry Margaret – us big kids will help you. There's lots of big kids.

Miss Dewson says it's very hard on your first day, but don't worry, it's just like school, only there's more of it, and when the bell rings you get to come here instead of going home. Now, Margaret, Margaret, d'you remember where everything is I showed you…there's the cloakroom where you come in, and the paste centre, and back there is the reading centre and the dress-up centre, and this is the free play area and the bathroom, and if you have to go I'll take you, Margaret, and this, Margaret, this is our Special Project Corner, and only one person's allowed here at a time, and usually it's just kids, and your brother is coming to get you at 5:30 so you don't have to worry, and you can stay with Miss Dewson…

special project area should include kids' drawings maybe have them done by a kindergarten group

perhaps Miss Dewson can always come from one area

Miss Dewson enters.

Miss Dewson: Janice, your Mom's here…Thanks for helping Margaret, Janice.

Janice: Bye, Miss Dewson…bye, Margaret.

Janice exits.

Miss Dewson: How was your first day, Margaret?…You like the duck eggs?… You can stay with them for a while, if you like?

I'm just over here if you want to ask me anything...

Miss Dewson exits leaving Margaret alone with the eggs.

Margaret looks off in various directions as we hear the confusion going on in her head.

maybe have taped voice done live by other kids

Taped voice of Margaret:

"Don't worry – my brother will be here at 5:30. The big kids. Big kids. Don't worry. Free play area. The bathroom... project...corner...I think it's my duty-day...duty-day...But there's no mother duck...no mother duck...no mother...no mother...no mother...no mother..."

Margaret's voice fades into the Chart Theme, and as the Chart changes to Wednesday, Day 13, Margaret exits, and Todd is seen entering the daycare.

SCENE TWO

Wednesday, Day 13. Todd walks into the daycare carrying his coat and school supplies as he says good-bye to Jake in the hall.

don't worry about clothing change – keep prop clothes extra as this is done in winter

Todd:	No trespassing, Jake! You can't come in here because it's private property, and you can't have a snack because you don't go to daycare, and I love it here because I don't have to go home with my Mommy. No crossing this door. I can play with all the other kids because my Dad says I can stay here until the middle of the night. I'm privileged, Jake, I'm really, really special...
Miss Dewson:	*(entering)* Hi, Todd! Snack's ready!
Todd:	*(climbing boxes and trying to ignore Miss Dewson)* Be bop, be bop...I'm going to the top, Captain...
Miss Dewson:	You're going to get very hungry by six o'clock, Todd.

Exits.

Todd:	*(continuing to climb boxes))* Up, up, up and away...
Miss Dewson:	*(calling from distance)* Todd...get down!
Todd:	Be bop, be bop, be bop, bop, bop...

Janice should have a sandwich with her

Janice runs in.

Janice:	Miss Dewson says she's not going to chase after you today – she says it's up to you. It's grape juice and peanut butter.

Janice exits.

Todd: *(calling after her)* My Daddy says he's coming at four today, and my Mommy doesn't let me eat peanut butter, and I'm allergic, and I hate bread.

                      Janice reenters with a peanut butter sandwich and a spray watering bottle.

Janice: Get down, Toddhead! I saved you a sandwich. Miss Dewson says you have to have some protein for your brain.

Todd: I'll punch the protein out, acid rain.

Janice: I'll punch the protein in, basid brain.

Todd: Out!

Janice: In!

Todd: Go away!

Janice: I'm Miss Dewson's helper today.

Todd: I hate school.

Janice: It's my turn.

Todd: Go away!

Janice: You're bad, Todd. I'm not going to be your friend.

Todd: I don't want you to be my friend.

Janice: Your bones won't grow.

Todd: They will so!

Janice: They'll shrink up into nothing.

                      Pause.

use a location relevant to your area

Tomorrow my Daddy's taking me to Ontario Place to go ice-skating and everything.

                      Janice is checking the eggs, turning them and spraying them with water.

Todd: Kids who water eggs are full of yoke.

Janice: Eat your sandwich, baby Todd.

Todd: My sandwich is resting.

Janice: I have to concentrate, Todd. I have to check the temperature's right on the thermometer.

Todd: They'll be really cute when they're born, right Janice?

Janice:	They'll be slimy at first, naughty Todd…then they'll be cuddly cute.
Todd:	Can I water them?
Janice:	NO!
Todd:	Can I, Janice?…I want a turn…
Janice:	Only one person on here at a time. It's a rule.
Todd:	Janice!
Janice:	No – you didn't come for snack.
Todd:	Janice!
Janice:	Eat your snack and I'll let you water one egg.
Todd:	I told you dumb ears – my sandwich is having a rest.
Janice:	You're a spoiled boy, Todd.
Todd:	Kids who water eggs are sandwiches anyway.

> *Janice continues to water the eggs as Todd breaks up his sandwich.*

Todd:	Here, give them this peanut butter in case they come early like my brother.
Janice:	You don't feed eggs, baby Todd.
Todd:	Well, you don't water them either. She's just giving you an activity so time can go quickly and she can go home and get a job she can get paid at.

> *Janice eats the sandwich.*

Janice:	You're so premature you shouldn't be born yet.
Todd:	*(grabbing the watering bottle)* That's because my Mother watered me with grape juice.
Janice:	If I was your Mother I'd water you with glue!
Todd:	If I was your Mother I'd water you with poo!
Janice:	Glue!
Todd:	Poo!
Janice:	Glue!
Todd:	Poo!
Janice:	Glue!

Todd:	Poo!
Both:	Glue Poo, Glue Poo, Glue Poo, Glue Poo…

They begin to wriggle around the space like fish.

Both:	Gluepoogluepoogluepoogluepoogluepoo…

They start laughing uncontrollably.

Janice:	You're silly, Todd!
Todd:	Quick! Open your armpits!

She does. He tickles her.

Janice:	Stop it!

Miss Dewson enters.

Miss Dewson:	*(calling as she comes in)* Todd, Todd…your Mommy just called to say that your Daddy can't pick you up at six today, but Jake's Mom is coming to get you instead…okay, love?

Miss Dewson exits.

Todd:	*(running off after her)* Can I have snack, Miss Dewson…can I have a peanut butter sandwich…can I?…can I?…

Janice is alone with the duck egg box. She starts tidying up the mess she and Todd have made. Alex pops up from inside a box.

Alex:	Hey, Janice the Manice – your old lady's here!
Janice:	Not my Dad?
Alex:	I said your Mom!

Alex disappears. As Janice exits moodily, we hear the Chart Theme which marks the change to Thursday, Day 14.

SCENE THREE

The chart rises to reveal Thursday, Day 14, and the Chart music leads into a rhythmic drum sequence which accompanies this box chase scene. The boxes are used like puppets, either manipulated by a pole backstage or moved magically by actors inside or behind them. The scene is choreographed as a daredevil, thrill-seeking sequence – lashing round corners, charges and knockabouts – all almost, but never quite, crashing into the egg box. At the end of this sequence, Todd pops out of a box.

Todd:	I'm bored, Miss Dewson. Can I go to the paint centre?

As Todd exits, inside his box we hear the Chart Theme, which marks the change to Friday, Day 15.

SCENE FOUR

The Chart rises to reveal Friday, Day 15 as Todd reenters from the opposite side and proceeds to climb a pile of boxes.

Todd: *(calling down from part way up the boxes)* I'm scared, Janice.

Janice: *(popping out of a box)* Then get down, Todd. Let's play wedding – you can be the bride and Shayna and Robert can be the taxi.

> *They disappear into the boxes as Margaret walks to the duck corner with the bottle. She looks into the box to check the thermometer and carefully drips small amounts of water onto the shells of the eggs. She counts silently with her fingers to the number nine. Alex comes running through, yelling across to a friend.*

Alex: Hey, Adam – wanna be my best friend? Hey, man – let's play space invaders – I'm Darth Vadar – come on, you blockhead or I'll blow you up…

> *He sets up a small box in football style and prepares to kick it as he chants in Adam's direction.*

Argo - Argo - Argo - Argo -   use a team relevant to your location

> *Miss Dewson steps from behind a corner.*

Miss Dewson: *(to Alex)* Don't even think about it!

Alex: Ahhhhhh!

Miss Dewson: And I think that Adam wants to play by himself today.

Alex: No, he doesn't, Teach!

Miss Dewson: Alex…

Alex: Yeah, Miss?

Miss Dewson: D'you have a problem today, Alex? D'you want to have a chat?

Alex: Well…like I just don't feel like talkin' today, ya know…How about I just have a quiet time by them eggs?

> *He has noticed Margaret.*

I could cool out beside them eggos, eh?

Miss Dewson: Well, okay – but Alex, when you've had time to think about it, let's have a talk, okay?

Alex: Like, I could help the new kid learn the ropes, Miss Dew.

Miss Dewson:	Alex...Alex...please don't forget it's only Margaret's fourth day here, and its her first time with the eggs, so remember the rule–
Alex:	Only one kid in the duck corner at a time.
Miss Dewson:	Right!
Alex:	You got it, Miss D.
Miss Dewson:	Miss what?
Alex:	Dewson.

Miss Dewson exits.

Alex:	See ya, Judy!
Miss Dewson:	See ya, Al!

Alex climbs onto a level above the duck corner overlooking Margaret.

Pause.

Alex: *(to Margaret)* Wanna be my best friend for five minutes?

Margaret keeps looking into the box.

What's yer name again?...Hey, kid, what's yer name?...Like... what ya waitin' for? Duck soup?

Pause.

Hey, want me to drive you home in my brand new gold car?

Pause.

Hey, can you hear me? I'm gonna test you for hearing.

Alex starts making sounds with his hands which Margaret begins to take notice of and turns into an imaginative game, finally making contact with Alex.

I'll tell you a secret. I got nine tiger's eggs at home. When they hatch, they'll probably eat cute little ducks probably.

Pause.

I was just jokin' ya!

Pause.

I'll be yer friend for five minutes if you'll give me some gum. My grade three teacher stole my gum and my baby sitter, Melanie's gonna make her pay for it. She's gonna make her give me the money for it. You got any gum in your cubby?

Pause.

They won't all live, ya know…my best friend, Zack, he's twelve, and I'm stronger than him, and he says them eggos is gonna die, and Zackie, he knows, and he said that Miss Dewsie and her daycare kids, they'd be lucky if two of them hatched! I don't like ducks anyway – I like lions. Hey, why don't ya hold them and feel their hearts beating, eh? BOOM-BOOM, BOOM-BOOM!

> *Alex jumps down into the duck corner. Margaret puts her hands over her ears.*

Alex: Hey, kid, wanna see me juggle…Throw me a couple of them eggs…C'mon, gimme one of them eggs…sunny-side up – c'mon kid, I'll show you how to juggle!

> *Margaret jumps up abruptly and lunges at Alex with a very aggressive sound (perhaps like a lion) and forces him off the duck area. Alex runs off. Margaret quickly counts the eggs again on her fingers, checks the temperature and gives them more water. Todd appears from a box.*

Todd: Hey, weirdhead, your brother's here.

> *Margaret places her animal friend, Robert, gently in the egg box and exits. As she exits we hear the Chart Theme and the Chart changes to reveal Monday, Day 18, as Janice and Todd enter.*

SCENE FIVE

> *Monday, Day 18. Janice and Todd come in carrying piles of outdoor clothing – snowsuits, gloves, scarves, boots, extra socks, etc.*

Janice: I'm sleeping over at my Dad's house tomorrow, and he's going to take me to City Hall to go skating and everything.

maybe oversize clothes to make dressing easier and to make them look more childlike in their antics

> *Miss Dewson hurries on zipping up her ski jacket.*

choose a relevant place

Miss Dewson: Hurry up, you two, or you'll miss outside time.

> *She exits.*

action takes place in front of the eggs

> *Throughout this scene both struggle with the awful task of dressing for winter outdoors, seriously tackling the problems at hand, but managing to get coats on upside down, arms in wrong arm holes, boots on wrong feet and so on.*

Janice:	My Mommy can't sleep so she takes pills, and sometimes they make her really cranky.
Todd:	If she wants to sleep she should close her eyes, and you could pat her back.
Janice:	If she wants to sleep she should ask my Dad back.

Pause.

Todd:	My Dad never sleeps – he meditates.
Janice:	My Mom's meditation runs out twice a week sometimes.

Pause.

Todd:	I like vitamin C.
Janice:	I hate sugar.
Todd:	Sugar is bad.
Janice:	Sugar is bad for the world.
Todd:	Yuck to sugar.
Janice:	Yuck.
Todd:	Yuck, Yuck.
Janice:	I hate chocolate.
Todd:	Chocolate is bad.
Janice:	Chocolate is worse than coffee.
Todd:	All the chocolate and sugar should be flushed down the toilet.
Janice:	We never eat sugar, right?
Todd:	Just at Christmas.
Janice:	Because our Grammas give us candies.
Todd:	Sugar's all right in candy.
Janice:	I love porridge anyway – even without sugar.
Todd:	If you love porridge you'll have to marry it.
Janice:	I'm going to marry my Dad.
Todd:	You can't marry your Dad – you're not allowed. It's a rule.
Janice:	I won't marry you anyway, that's for sure.
Todd:	I don't want to get married, anyway. I'm going to be a monk.
Janice:	You're an immature boy, Todd.

Todd:	I wouldn't marry you anyway.
Janice:	I wouldn't marry you if you were the last man on earth.
Todd:	I'm a boy anyway.
Janice:	Girls are better than boys – you're a boy, YUCK!
Todd:	Boys are better than girls – and you're a girl, YUCK!
Janice:	Boys are yuck!
Todd:	Girls are yuck!

Pause.

Janice:	You're not very smart, you know. Miss Dewson told me to help you with your snow suit, baby boo ba.
Todd:	If I were grown up, I'd put all the girls in jars.
Janice:	But you're not – you're just a baby boo ba, and anyway I'm in grade two.
Todd:	You're going to fail and everything, you know.
Janice:	You should go to slow camp, Todd…I'm going to tell Miss Dewson that you should go to slow camp…They can teach you to put your boots on at slow camp…I'm going to tell Miss Dewson that you should go to slow camp…
Todd:	You're nagging at me! You're nagging!
Janice:	You're boring my ears off.
Todd:	Your Daddy should spank you.
Janice:	My Daddy doesn't live with me, so there!
Todd:	You're a single parent family, so there!
Janice:	You're WILD.
Todd:	You're BOSSY.
Janice:	You're a…VEGETARIAN!

Pause.

Todd:	When my children grow up, they'll all eat seaweed.
Janice:	And there'll be no more wars.
Todd:	Wars are really bad.
Janice:	I don't like violence, do you?
Todd:	Violence is bad. We have Pay T.V. – it's obscene. Sometimes

when I'm good my Daddy lets me watch violence until midnight, except when my little brother tricks me into smashing him.

Pause.

Everyone gets violent sometimes.

Janice:	My Mother gets migraines.
Todd:	She should go to my Dad's classes. He teaches meditation.
Janice:	I KNOW, STUPID PIG!
Todd:	You're not a very nice person, Janice.
Janice:	Yes, I am.
Todd:	It hurts my feelings when you call me stupid pig.
Janice:	It hurts my feelings when my Dad doesn't take me skating.

Pause.

Todd:	I'm going to be a mountain climber, you know.
Janice:	And I'll write you letters, Todd.
Todd:	I'll climb all the mountains in the world and everything.
Janice:	And I'll wave to you, Todd.
Todd:	I'll be famous.
Janice:	I know you will, Todd.
Todd:	And we'll get an apartment.
Janice:	I'd never marry Alex.
Todd:	Alex is bad.
Janice:	He's naughty.
Todd:	He talks funny.
Janice:	He doesn't tidy up.
Todd:	He's going to be my best friend tomorrow.
Janice:	He's not going to marry anyone – he's going to have tattoos.
Todd:	And a motorcycle.
Janice:	He's eight and a half.
Todd:	He's eight and three-quarters.
Janice:	My Dad's over twenty.

Todd:	Your Mom's a pillhead.
Janice:	Your Mom's a pillow.
Todd:	Your Dad's a blanket.
Janice:	Your Dad's a cushion.
Todd:	Your cushion's a brother.
Janice:	Your cushion's a mother.
Todd:	Oh, brother.
Janice:	Oh, brother.
Todd:	Oh, brother.
Janice:	Oh, brother.

depending upon the set of the boxes, the two may be able to walk in caravan style over them as they gradually get dressed so they are not in one place too long

have one direction as being outside

They are now doing a stomping dance.

Both: Oh, brother. Oh, brother. Oh, brother. Oh, brother...

Both are now fully dressed. They can hardly move and are completely buried in winter's paraphernalia. We see four eyes and two noses. Janice and Todd are jumping around in an ungainly fashion as Miss Dewson enters, unzipping her ski jacket.

Miss Dewson: Too late, you two – you missed outside time – take your snowsuits off.

Miss Dewson exits. Todd and Janice freeze. They start wandering off with some difficulty.

Janice: What does a 500 pound duck say?

Todd: I dunno.

Janice: *(in basso profundo)* QUACK, QUACK!

Todd: Oh, brother!

As they exit, we hear the Chart Theme and the Chart changes to reveal Tuesday, Day 19, while we see Margaret entering from the opposite side.

SCENE SIX

a large clock is more easily seen

Tuesday, Day 19. Margaret walks to the egg box concealing something she has brought from home. We hear the sound of ticking which vaguely resembles a heartbeat. She has brought a watch and places it beside the eggs. She counts the nine eggs on her fingers. As Margaret exits, Alex comes racing in, playing with a box, followed by Todd.

Todd: I'll be your best friend, Alex – I'll be your best friend.

Alex: Okay, great – hold this.

                Handing Todd a box.

                Wanna play spy? Okay, what we need is camouflage…

Todd: *(they whisper conspiratorially)* Camouflage, yeah!

Alex: *(covering Todd with boxes)* Okay, this is great camouflage – now freeze – don't move – okay!

                Alex runs off, leaving Todd covered in boxes. After about ten seconds, Alex, with Janice, pops up from a box on the opposite side of the set. They are giggling hysterically.

Alex: What a weirdo!

                They disappear. Todd gets out of the boxes. He checks to see if anyone is looking.

Todd: I'm not your friend, Alex – I'll never be your best friend.

                Exiting.

                As Todd exits we hear the Chart Theme and the Chart changes to reveal Wednesday, Day 20. At the same time, Margaret comes running in on one side and Alex on the other.

SCENE SEVEN

Wednesday, Day 20. Margaret enters from one side wearing a box on her head. Alex enters from the opposite side wearing a box on his head. They meet in the middle. A game develops which both enjoy. During the game Alex disappears into the boxes. Margaret is left searching for him. Todd appears. Todd walks into the duck corner with the watering bottle. Margaret watches from a distance as Todd sprinkles water on the eggs.

Todd: Hi, Margaret!

                Pause.

Todd: Hey, d'you want to see me climb up? I'm not scared, you know! I can get almost to the top!

                He piles up boxes against one of the highest boxes.

                Be bop, be bop, be bop…

Miss Dewson: *(calling from a distance)* Todd – Get down!

                Margaret walks closer to the egg box. Todd descends.

                Pause.

Todd:	You shouldn't have left that watch there, Margaret. That's a rule, you know!

Todd is aware that he is getting no response from Margaret.

Todd:	Can you talk, Margaret?...Margaret?...
	QUACK! QUACK!

Margaret looks up at him momentarily.

Pause.

Todd:	BOO!

Pause.

Todd:	It's time you said something, Margaret, so say something... say...BELLY BUTTON!

Todd tries a different tactic. He starts running on the spot.

Todd:	Okay, Margaret, running on the spot – track team, right? Okay, running on the spot – knees up – hup two, hup two. Here, Margaret, here, now turn around, turn around...

Margaret has joined him and is tentatively running on the spot. She turns around, and Todd bumps her with his bum making a silly noise. After doing this several times, he's got her laughing but not talking.

Todd:	*(stopping in mid-bump)* Okay, Margaret, okay. Sit down, Margaret.

She gets a box.

Right, now I'm your talking teacher, okay? Okay! Now, it's very important for people to talk. Do you understand? Raise your hand if you don't understand.

Margaret raises her hand. She is having a problem sitting on the box.

Okay, this is how you talk – put your hand down, Margaret – now you move your tongue, okay – and your lips –

He blows through his lips.

Then you make a sound – AAAAAAAAAHHHHHHHHHH – then you grab onto the sound with your lips – ahbuh, ahbuh – buh, buh, buh, buh – understand?

Margaret puts her hand up.

Okay, try it – except instead of saying "ahbuh," you can make words – like "YOGURT." Say "YOGURT," Margaret, c'mon try it – put you hand down, Margaret. Okay, push the sound out of your throat and grab onto "YOGURT." C'mon – "YOOOOOOOOOGURRRRRRT! YOGURT!" You're not even trying, Margaret!

Out of frustration, Todd decides to attempt the old armpit tactic to try tickling her into talking.

Todd: Okay, Margaret, quick, open your armpits –

She doesn't.

Open your armpits!

She doesn't.

Quick – open!

Margaret: Nooooooooooo!

Janice and Alex fly on in a wonderful two-headed bird.

very bright in colour
use real feathers in head
if possible, cut arm holes
under wings to allow the
occupants to flap, should
be spectacular by a child's
definition
the two heads could be
the two actors

Todd: She talks! She talks! She talks! Miss Dewson, it's wonderful! She talks!

Todd, Janice and Alex fly off to spread the amazing news.

All Three: She talks! She talks! She talks! Caw! Caw!

Margaret is left alone on the stage with the duck eggs.

Margaret: (to the egg) How come everyone wants me to talk around here…You're new here and I've never even heard you cheep, ever.. Belly button!…Yogurt!!!

She is very undecided about what to do next. Finally, she picks up Todd's forgotten watering bottle.

Margaret: It's…sure…strange…around here…boy!

She kicks a box in a gesture of defiance and runs off. From this point on, whenever she sees Todd, she is likely to put up her hand. As Margaret exits, we hear the Chart Theme and the Chart changes to Thursday, Day

21. At the same time, we see Janice enter wearing a "Boring Pigeon" box.

SCENE EIGHT

all one colour (dull gray/mauve), dull features painted on

Thursday, Day 21. There is a "Caw" from behind Janice. She turns. A magnificent hawk wing flutters for a second out of a box. Another "Caw." She turns. A wing on a pole flies high above the boxes. Another "Caw." She turns, but Alex flies in behind her in a magnificent hawk box, followed by Margaret. He swoops through the space. Margaret hovers unobtrusively at one side, enjoying the show.

Alex: Caw! Caw! Caw!

Janice watches enviously.

Todd enters. Alex takes off his box and runs over to Todd.

Alex: Hey, Toddhead, I'll be your best friend, okay?

Todd: I'm not stupid, Alex. All you do is play dumb tricks on me. I'm not stupid, you know.

Alex: Yeah, I know – gee, I'm sorry – and we was gonna be partners.

Todd: Partners, Alex?

Alex: Yeah, gangster partners.

Todd: You and me, gangster partners!

Alex: Yeah, but first we gotta bust outa jail!

Todd: Okay, Joe...

They both start talking in "gangsterese" as Alex proceeds to erect a jail of boxes around Todd.

Alex: Okay, Mike – now this is the jail, right – now, I'm gonna give ya the password to bust out, right – now don't move till I give ya the word...

Margaret, half-concealed behind some boxes, watches with increasing alarm the following events. Janice has been eyeing the magnificent hawk box. She has taken off her pigeon wings and goes to put on the hawk. Alex stops in mid-construction, leaving Todd completely surrounded by boxes.

Alex: Janice...Janice, you leave that alone. It's mine, so you give it to me right now.

Janice: It's a rule that if you stop playing with something the other person can use it.

Alex:	I don't care about no rules – gimme it!
Janice:	Well, yesterday you said you'd be my best friend and you aren't.
Alex:	Yeah…so write a letter to the principal…big deal!
Janice:	You're mean, Alex.
Alex:	Well, you're really ugly, Janice – so gimme that right now or I'll smash you!
Janice:	It's mine now – you left it.
Alex:	Give it to me – now.
Janice:	It's mine.
Alex:	It's not yours, it's the school's. I'm gonna smash you.
Janice:	No hitting, stupid – I'll tell Miss Dewson on you.
Alex:	Give me it…

He pushes her and they both start pulling at the box. Todd bursts out of the boxes.

Todd:	I'm going to tell Miss Dewson that you can't even share. You're boring my ears off…*(as he exits)* I'm going to te-el, I'm going to te-el, I'm going to te-el.

Pause.

Alex and Janice think about Miss Dewson coming and decide to try different means.

Alex:	I need it, eh!…my best friend, Zack, I'll get him to give you a quarter for it.
Janice:	I get ten dollars a week allowance. I don't need money like you need money.
Alex:	You need some brains, dummy…Hey, Janice the Manice, Janice the Manice, Janice the Manice.
Janice:	Why don't you just go to jail where you belong.
Alex:	Gimme it, Janice, it's mine.
Janice:	No.
Alex:	I'll smash this stoopid thing…
Janice:	Nobody likes you, Alex.

Alex:	Nobody likes you 'cause you're snotty.
Janice:	Everyone hates you 'cause you smell.
Alex:	I hate you, Janice.
Janice:	That's a bad word and I'm telling on you.

They have now forgotten about Miss Dewson and are yelling very loudly.

Alex:	SNOTTY!
Janice:	SMELLY!
Alex:	SNOTTY!
Janice:	SMELLY!
Alex:	SNOTTY!
Janice:	SMELLY!

The magnificent hawk box is now being torn to shreds in the tussle.

Alex:	Gimme it...it's MINE!...MINE!...MINE!
Janice:	You'll never have it...EVER - EVER - EVER...

wings, head and tail can be retaped so try to preserve the body of the box

Miss Dewson enters.

Miss Dewson:	ALEX...JANICE...THAT'S ENOUGH!
Alex:	*(running off)* I hate this place.

The box is totally demolished. Janice is looking at it.

Miss Dewson:	Janice?

Janice walks over to her pigeon box, tears it up and runs off.

Miss Dewson:	*(following her off)* Janice!

We hear a faint sound of heartbeats coming from the egg box as the Chart Theme begins to mark the transition into Friday, Day 22. Margaret, now alone, quickly checks the egg box and slips out.

begin to slowly increase the heartbeats throughout the remainder of the play

SCENE NINE

Friday, Day 22. This is one instance where the Chart Theme reflects a very distinct change in mood. Before its completion, we see four heads peering cautiously around boxes towards the egg incubation box. Janice and Alex slip out of sight. Margaret walks slowly on, carrying the watering bottle. She is followed by Todd. The mood is one of grave sensationalism. Two of the eggs were found cracked and broken this morning. They have been removed. The two children approach the egg box apprehensively. They count the eggs.

use dimmer lighting

Both: One, two, three, four, five, six, SEVEN...

Pause.

Todd: You mustn't be sad, Margaret. It's survival of the fittest. That's a law you know.

Margaret: I would have carried them everywhere even if they couldn't have waddled.

Todd: But they wouldn't have been happy if they couldn't have waddled.

Pause.

Todd: The janitor found them this morning.

Margaret: They're dead.

Todd: All cracked up.

Margaret: I'll miss them, Todd, won't you?

Todd: I was going to carry them to the very top when I'm big enough to get there.

Margaret: I was going to watch them swim.

Todd: He just found them there this morning – the janitor.

Margaret: Two dead.

Todd: All squashed up.

Margaret: What do you think happened?

Todd: Maybe they were murdered!

At this thought the children remove themselves from the duck box area and confer at a distance.

Margaret: Who did it?

Todd: Could have been the janitor.

Margaret: Or the Grade Fours.

Todd: It could have been the Grade Fours.

Margaret: Maybe a book fell on them.

Todd:	It could have.
Margaret:	Maybe they just had weak shells – maybe the noise cracked them.
Todd:	Maybe God did it.
Margaret:	Why would God do it?
Todd:	He might have pushed them by mistake.
Margaret:	But God's everywhere – he could have caught them. Why do things have to die, Todd?

They have returned slowly to a level above the duck box.

Margaret:	*(counting the eggs)* one, two, three, four, five, six, seven…

To Todd.

	You mustn't be sad though – it's a law, and don't be sad when you're lying in bed.
Todd:	I'm not sad. You can't be sad if it's a law.

Pause.

Margaret:	But seven is a very lucky number.

Pause.

Margaret:	Are you scared, Todd? D'you want to sleep over at my house?
Todd:	No – I'm not going home tonight. I'm staying here all night to guard the eggs.
Margaret:	You're not allowed. Your Mommy and Daddy won't let you.
Todd:	They're busy – they're not coming tonight.
Margaret:	What about the janitor?
Todd:	I'll hide.

Margaret rushes around and finds a very big box. Todd is talking to the duck eggs.

Todd:	Don't worry, duckies, don't worry – just think about the good things – just think about when you burst out all yellow with feathers and go flying zoom up to the top, and don't think about those other two dead ducks. Just think about poking out of your shells and being born and having adventures and stuff…
Margaret:	Hide under this box.

Todd gets under the box. He reappears for a second.

Todd: *(to the eggs)* Think about it!

                       He hides. Margaret starts to tiptoe off. Miss Dewson enters.

Miss Dewson: *(calling as she enters)* Todd…Todd…

                       There is no sign of Todd. A large box sits prominently centre stage.

Miss Dewson: *(to box)* Your Daddy's here.

                       Exits.

                       Pause.

                       After a few seconds, as Margaret watches in dismay, Todd flings off the box.

Todd: *(calling to his Dad in an attempt to lure him to the scene of the crime and to relate the day's terrible events.)* Daddy, Daddy, two of the ducks got squashed and everything – and Alex probably murdered them – and the janitor found their little wee bodies all cracked up at the bottom, and it's been an awful day, and I've been here alone, and I've been very sad, just crying and crying, and all the other kids have gone home except me…

Miss Dewson: *(reentering and interrupting him midstream)* Get your coat… Todd…get your coat.

                       Todd exits. Margaret is standing by the egg box. She is very upset.

Miss Dewson: Margaret…

                       As Miss Dewson leads Margaret off, we hear the unmistakable rhythm of a heartbeat, which leads into the Chart Theme marking the change into Monday, Day 25.

SCENE TEN

                       Monday, Day 25. Janice enters with the watering bottle. She has been more affected, perhaps, than any child at the daycare by the duck egg loss. She bends down to water the eggs and seems to be tense with concentration and concern when Margaret and Todd suddenly enter. They are in a state of excitement.

Todd: I've got strategy, Janice, strategy!

                       Margaret raises her hand.

                       Yes, Margaret?

Margaret: I – I had this dream last night, Todd… I – I dreamed – I dreamed there was eggs under my pillow – and – and – if I put

	my head on my pillow they would all crack…it really made me sweat!
Todd:	Janice, we're having a meeting about the ducks. We've got to protect the few remaining ducks.

Margaret raises her hand.

Yes, Margaret?

Margaret:	Probably – probably they're thinking – who's next!
Todd:	Two down – seven to go!
Janice:	This is a club, okay! This is our club, okay!
Todd:	I'm the General! You two are Captains!

Margaret raises her hand.

Yes, Captain Margaret?

Margaret:	My finger's cracked today. Maybe it's a disease.
Janice:	Okay, this is our club, okay! How are we going to protect the eggs, General?
Todd:	I got strategy and everything, Captain Janice.

Margaret raises her hand.

Yes, Captain?

Margaret:	The sooner they get out of here the better for them…They should jump out the window and…fly to a farm.
Todd:	Okay, strategy number one…BUILD A FORT TO PROTECT THE DUCKS!

During the next few exchanges, the children are urgently building a fort out of boxes, sealing off an area around the duck box.

Todd:	I'm the 'outside guard,' and you be the 'inside guard,' Captain Janice. I'm having a gun.

He finds a piece of cardboard for this purpose.

Janice:	Guns aren't allowed.

Margaret raises her hand.

Yes, Margaret?

Todd:	Yes, Captain?

Todd keeps his rifle.

Margaret:	I'll beat on this drum, Sir...to – to keep away...evil spirits...

From this point on, she beats a rhythm which gets more and more intense throughout the scene.

They have completed the fort and take up positions.

Todd:	Strategy number two – don't let anyone near the fort!

They begin to practice their various duck guard procedures. Alex enters. Janice emits a warning siren noise. Margaret beats rapidly on her drum.

Alex:	Hey, what ya got here...Hey, that's really great...Can I play Toddhead?
Todd:	Not allowed.
Janice:	Go away.
Todd:	No trespassing.
Alex:	Hey, c'mon – I'll be the enemy line.

Alex starts to build something from the few remaining boxes.

Janice:	My Dad says not to play with you because you're too rough.
Alex:	So what...I'm king of this daycare anyways, and your Dad's a weirdo...
Janice:	You think you're Batman, but you're not.
Todd:	Private property – go away.

He kicks over Alex's boxes.

Janice:	It's a club – you're not allowed.
Todd:	Go away, dumb Alex.
Janice:	Not allowed! Not allowed!
Alex:	C'mon you guys...
Todd:	You never let me play with you anyways, and you always trick me, and anyways we're guarding our duck eggs, and you don't even like eggs, and anyways you're too rough!
Alex:	I like eggs.

Janice and Todd start chanting.

Both:	YOU'RE TOO ROUGH! YOU'RE TOO ROUGH! YOU'RE TOO ROUGH! YOU'RE TOO ROUGH!

Alex approaches the fort to knock it down. Margaret's voice is heard above the others.

Margaret: ALEX KILLS DUCKS!

For a second all four stop dead in their tracks. Then Janice, Todd and later Margaret pick up the new chant with double force.

ALEX KILLS DUCKS!
ALEX KILLS DUCKS!
ALEX KILLS DUCKS!
ALEX KILLS DUCKS!
ALEX KILLS DUCKS!

Miss Dewson enters.

Miss Dewson: THAT'S ENOUGH!

Alex exits in tears.

Miss Dewson: Alex didn't touch the eggs. Tidy up these boxes and come into the other room!

Miss Dewson exits after Alex.

Todd, Janice and Margaret slowly clear the space of the boxes. Todd and Margaret exit. Janice is about to leave but goes quickly to check the eggs. She is almost in tears.

Janice: I don't know if all of you will make it, and I don't know what you'll be like, but I sure hope all of you make it.

Janice exits as we hear the sound of heartbeats, more insistent than before, followed by the Chart Theme, which marks the change into Tuesday, Day 26, as Alex runs on.

SCENE ELEVEN

Tuesday, Day 26. Alex has obviously not recovered from the events of the day before. He addresses the duck eggs.

Alex: I always get the blame. I'm always the bad guy…Well, I don't care, 'cause I didn't touch no eggs, and anyway I really hate you guys, and I just wish you'd get born and get outta here.

Alex climbs onto a high box away from the playing area. He picks up a drum box.

Alex: I don't care if they think I smashed them eggs 'cause I didn't, and even if I go to jail I didn't, and I'm never goin' to talk to anyone in this dumb daycare ever again…

He starts to drum like a rock star. He is in fact an accomplished drummer. Margaret enters. She sees Alex. Margaret moves towards him.

Margaret: Alex?

Alex stops drumming but continues to mime the action, as if shutting Margaret out by not letting her hear. She backs off. Alex starts drumming again.

Margaret: Alex?

She approaches him again. Alex mimes drumming. Margaret backs off. He resumes real drumming.

Margaret: Alex?

Alex mimes drumming.

Margaret: I only wanted to say I'm sorry – I know you didn't murder those eggs.

She runs off. Alex resumes drumming with a passion. Janice pops out of a box.

Janice: Alex?

Alex throws down his drum and runs off. Janice disappears. Rapid heartbeats lead into the Chart Theme to mark the change to Wednesday, Day 27. Alex is seen running on from the other side.

SCENE TWELVE

Alex's space should be fairly high up so that the group is removed from him
it makes movement patterns easier as well

Wednesday, Day 27. Alex enters. Janice, Todd and Margaret peep out from behind various boxes and watch him. He returns to his "drumming corner." The other three vanish from sight. Alex starts drumming. They peep out again. Alex does not see them. They signal to each other and exit. Alex continues to drum.

Todd enters bearing a large piece of cardboard, zooming into the space like an express train. He lays it down and begins to break dance on it in time to Alex's drums. Alex ignores him.

Margaret and Janice enter. They also start dancing. As they do, all three start to move towards him. Now Alex starts the old miming trick. Each time he does so the other three freeze. Gradually, they ease very close indeed. Then, instead of freezing, they take up the drumming and drum on themselves, on each other, on the floor, on boxes. This produces the giggles and eventually all four are drumming wildly. They pick up a rhythm in unison, which they vocalize as they dance around, four friends again.

All:	Dadadadumdadadadumdadadadum…

Miss Dewson enters. She sees that all is well. She exits. At the climax of the dance they collapse in laughter.

Alex: Hey, you guys, I've got an idea…

He leads them on all fours around the duck box in some sort of ritualistic "Salute to the Eggs"…

Alex: Shhhhh!

Everybody: Shhhhhhhhhhhhhhhhh!

There is much hugging and hilarity. The four friends are reunited. They dance off together led by Alex. We hear rapid heartbeats, which lead into the Chart Theme to mark the transition into Thursday, Day 28.

SCENE THIRTEEN

Thursday, Day 28. There is an edgy feeling in the daycare today. Everyone is waiting impatiently for the eggs to hatch. We see all four children in various places on the set. All seem preoccupied with their separate worlds. Todd has climbed up higher than ever before. Margaret is sitting with the eggs. Alex is occupying a box with a lid like a Jack-in-a-box. Janice is huddled inside a little house box.

Margaret: *(to the eggs)* My Mommy said I can wear my new shoes in case you come early. If you come late everyone's going to be really cross.

bows should be quite large and in a colour similar to her costume

Miss Dewson: *(from a distance)* TODD – GET DOWN!

Janice: I just wish they'd get on with it…I'm fed up with waiting for those eggs to hatch!

Alex: Fed up! Fed up!

Miss Dewson: *(calling from off)* TODD – GET DOWN AT ONCE – YOU'RE NOT BIG ENOUGH TO CLIMB UP THERE YET!

Todd clambers down.

Margaret: If you come really late, my shoes aren't going to be new any more.

Janice: If this is what it's like having babies…it's really BORING!

Todd: I'm bored with having to get DOWN all the time.

Alex: Boring! Boring!

Margaret:	Alex didn't smash your brother and sister, you know. Miss Dewson said it was an accident in nature.
Janice:	Let's play Superwoman!
Todd:	That's boring.
Janice:	We could play wedding?
Todd:	No!
Margaret:	My Mommy says I can wear my new shoes on special occasions…
Todd:	When are those eggs going to get BORN. That's what I want to know.
Alex:	Probably next Christmas, Toddhead!
Margaret:	And it'll be a special occasion when you're born, that's why I can wear them.
Janice:	I'm going to ask Miss Dewson to make those eggs hurry up!
	She exits.
Todd:	I'll get to the very top of you – someday!
	He exits.
Margaret:	My shoes are pink – with bows.

perhaps dark shoes with pink bows would be simpler

Alex walks over to join Margaret by the eggs.

Alex:	Eggs is born every minute all over the world without boring kids hanging around watching them, you know…and they don't even have a mother…Where's their mother, then?… Them ducks must feel pretty dumb bein' born in a box in a daycare with no mother. You gonna marry them or some-thing?…The whole thing makes me sick, I tell ya…'cause if I see one more dumb kid gaping at some dumb eggs, I'm just gonna be bored to sick!

Alex starts to exit.

Margaret:	*(calling after him)* I'll be your best friend, Alex!

They run off together. We hear very rapid and insistent heart-beats, followed by the final Chart Theme to mark the change into Friday, Day 29.

SCENE FOURTEEN

fanfare could be used to mark the start of the last day

Friday, Day 29. Margaret, Janice and Alex run on and gather round the egg box. They freeze in action. The staging of this scene is stylized. The action on stage is frozen in time and space, while the hatching of the ducklings is dramatized by the voices of many children on tape. This tape has almost the quality of a greek chorus – a rhythmic and suspenseful drive building towards a climax.

Adam: Come on, little fella, come on, come on...

Alice: Come on, little fella...

Robert: Look...

Alice: Come on...

Shayna: Come on...

Ruth: Come on, Nellie...

Sam: It's going to hatch...it's going to hat...

Several Voices: LOOK!

if more bodies are available at this point, use more kids and keep the primary actors in their own special space

> *A slight gasp.*

Adam: There's another big crack, Miss Dewson.

Robert: It's stretching.

perhaps the extras could cluster around the box making the audience want to see inside

Ruth: It's moving, it's moving...

Several Voices: LOOK!

> *A slight scream from the group.*

Adam: HE POKED A HOLE!

Alice: I think it's a duck.

Sam: I think they're both ducks.

Shayna: I see a beak.

Adam: COME ON, LITTLE FELLA...

Alice: It's a black one, a black one...

Sam: I can't see, Robert...

Robert: Shut up...

Ruth: Come on, Nellie...

Alice: It's poking, it's poking...

Several Voices: IT'S POKING.

> *A slightly bigger scream. Silence.*
>
> *Pause.*

Shayna:	I'm scared…
Robert:	Maybe we're being too noisy…
Frank:	I've got an earache…
Ruth:	It's not poking…
Miss Dewson:	It's just having a quiet time…
Shayna:	It's sucking in the last bit of its yuk…
Sam:	I feel like ripping the rest of its shell off..
Robert:	I feel like helping…
Ruth:	I feel like sticking in and pullingit out.
Sam:	Maybe it needs a little push…
Ruth:	PUSH!
Several Voices:	PUSH…PUSH…
Joyce:	It's really black, Miss Dewson.
Shayna:	Come on, Blackie…
Sam:	Come on, Yellow…
Robert:	Blackie doesn't give up…
Frank:	I'm betting on Yellow…
Several Voices:	Come on, come on, come on, little fella…
Miss Dewson:	He's almost out!
Robert:	IT'S COMING…

*The chorus of children's voices now coaxes the ducks on during
the final stretch with duck sounds.*

Children's Voices:

QUACK!
QUACK!
QUACK!
QUACK!
QUACK!
QUACK!
QUACK!
QUACK!
QUACK!

*make sure that Todd's
climbing does not steal
focus from the hatching
maybe he can do it
from behind*

*This chorus crescendos into a final cheer and a round of
applause. At this the three children on stage become animated.*

> *We see Todd appear, towering on the very top of the highest box. The tape stops.*

Janice: She did it! She did it! She did it! SHE DID IT! TODD!

Alex: *(still staring in awe and amazement at the egg box)* WOW…Oh, WOW…that was great…Boy, you did just great…Wow, slurping out, like alive and everything…all slimy and alive…Good for you, duck! Good for you, Duckie! Boy, wait till I tell old Zacko about this…he'll be really knocked out. Boy, that duck is great…excellentissimo, kiddo!

Margaret: She made it, Todd, and I'm wearing my new shoes. She pushed as hard as she could and she came out, Todd…She poked and she poked and she poked, and then she got born because she wanted to be alive so much, and I'm wearing my new shoes… isn't that great?

Todd: *(calling from the very top)* Okay, duckie…just open your armpits – open your armpits and flap…You can do it, duckie…I did it… Come on, you can do it…just open your armpits and FLY…that's what wings are for! I did it, come on up…open your armpits and FLY…

Alex: *(taking over the situation)* I think she should have a rest first, Todd…I think she should have a rest.

Todd: Yeah, maybe she should…

> *The children start tiptoeing out as if in the presence of a newborn baby. Todd climbs down from his tower. Just before they exit, they turn back to the duck box.*

Todd: HAPPY BIRTHDAY, DUCKIE!

All: *(as they run off)* HAPPY BIRTHDAY, DUCKIE!

The End

End ideas
Have a chorus of Happy Birthday, with musical accompaniment, that includes the audience
have the set open after the show for climbing on by the audience
have the calendar do something special at the end of the show

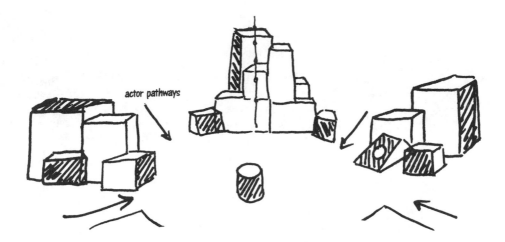

Box ideas

Use some stronger wooden boxes as the framework for the mountain of boxes. The height of the piles of boxes combined with the colours should form a vibrant background to the action. If designs are desired on the boxes (ie, rocket pictures), have children paint them; however, solid-colour boxes leave more to the audience's imagination. Keep some of the boxes solid, have others with openings at one or both ends. Boxes should be stacked on top of each other in front of strong support structures. The set could begin as a uniform adult world and gradually be turned into the chaotic, colourful world of the children.

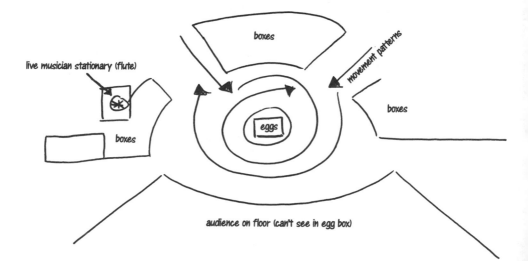

Action ideas

The play moves and changes fast; entrances and exits should be large to accommodate accelerated motion. It's more exciting if the action can surround the audience; extra sound besides the human element may also add to the thrill (on tape maybe). Use extra bodies whenever necessary to create a larger sense of the space of the centre and the overwhelming energy of the children; however, keep in mind that a younger audience is very easily distracted by too much long-term excitement.

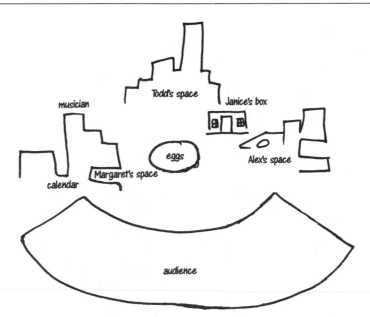

If several of the boxes are very large, they can be used as homes for the actors with each actor having his own space

Option for a set in a smaller room – use a corner

The calendar

Use a live calendar

Ideas
Three people for the calendar:
two dancers wearing black as mimes,
one calendar with good facial expression
who is stationary

Work out themes for the change (ie, winter snowball fight, Laurel and Hardy, hide and seek, snow angels). Calendar could move out during scene changes, then back to the same space. At some points, a problem may occur with the accumulation of boxes within the necessary acting space. The calendar could be choreographed to move the boxes, the calendar music could reflect the emotions of the previous scene while blending into an introduction for the next. Investigate ideas on soundscape – if the troupe of performers is loud enough, experienced musicians may not be completely necessary. The length of time for each calendar scene may be dependent upon the previous daytime scene – it can be used as a calm-down after a very busy scene or vice-versa depending upon the presumed attention span of the audience. Taking more time with the calendar scene uses more people as performers, allows actors enough time to get props, focuses the audience's attention constantly upon the upcoming event.

Calendar may also be hand puppets

Egg box

Isolate egg box by overhead yellow light or make the incubator box bright yellow
If light is unavailable, tape a line on the floor that only the helper is allowed to cross

About the Editor

JOYCE DOOLITTLE is a teacher, director, actress, author and longtime advocate of children's theatre. She has acted in and directed over one hundred plays for academic, community and professional theatres, including many for young people. She is Professor Emeritus of Drama at the University of Calgary, where she introduced courses in creative drama and theatre for young audiences. From 1966 to 1979 she represented Canada at the Association International du Théâtre pour l'Enfants et la Jeunesse, the world organization for theatre for children and youth. She coauthored, with Zina Barnieh, *A Mirror of Our Dreams: Children and Theatre in Canada* (Talonbooks, 1979) and edited *Eight Plays for Young People* (NeWest Press, 1984). She founded Calgary's Pumphouse Theatre, a renovated water pumping station containing two flexible performing spaces, one of which is named in her honour. Joyce Doolittle has received an Alberta Achievement Award and the Cohen Award for outstanding contribution to theatre.

About the Designers

Tara Ryan

TARA RYAN received her Bachelor of Fine Arts from the University of Calgary and is currently at work on a Bachelor of Education, paths which reflect her two loves – the theatre and teaching. Her future plans include further theatre study in Asia and teaching in northern Alberta Native communities.

Douglas McCullough

DOUGLAS MCCULLOUGH is Professor of Drama at the University of Calgary and a professional designer and fine artist. He has designed more than one hundred academic and professional productions in Canada and the United States, including industrial shows, performance art, theatre, opera, ballet, contemporary dance and children's theatre.

James Andrews

JAMES ANDREWS teaches Lighting Design and Technical Theatre at the University of Calgary to both undergraduate and graduate students. He also designs lighting for academic and professional theatre productions.

About the Plays

A Nest of Dragons
ZINA BARNIEH

A prince with a penchant for raising unusual pets discovers that some wild things cannot be tamed. Through the trials of a journey, his youthful passion is transformed into a more mature attachment and attitude.

The Old Woman and the Pedlar
BETTY JANE WYLIE

When an old woman sleeping beside a road has her skirts cut off by a mischievous pedlar, she wakes to a problem. With her appearance changed, she faces an identity crisis, and she must seek the assistance of fantastic strangers to rediscover her name.

The Merchants of Dazu
JAMES DEFELICE

Two unscrupulous adventurers are driven by dreams of great wealth on a journey during which they exploit the innocence of the peasants they encounter. But they receive their comeuppance when, threatened by ill weather and rough terrain on the return trip, they must turn to those same peasants in an effort to survive.

Prairie Dragons
SHARON POLLOCK

Two teenaged heroines face prejudice that denies them equal opportunities to succeed. Their story is told by a dragon – a prairie dragon, brought by Chinese immigrants, that can bring good fortune to those who are true to themselves and their vision.

Swimmers
CLEM MARTINI

Two improbable friends imagine a world of only water, but this environment turns into an unexpected nightmare until they begin to face reality and better understand the nature of friendship.

Friends
TOM BENTLEY-FISHER

Children in a daycare use boxes to create houses, cars, rockets and more as they prepare for a miracle of birth – the hatching of a nest of ducks. The event serves as a catalyst to the characters' understanding of both their growing independence and continuing interdependence.